The Flowers Along the Way

The Flowers Along the Way

A Memoir

CLAUDIA CASTRO LUNA

CURBSTONE BOOKS / NORTHWESTERN UNIVERSITY PRESS
EVANSTON, ILLINOIS

Northwestern University Press
www.nupress.northwestern.edu

The names of some individuals have been altered to protect their identities.

The epigraph on page 51 is from a homily delivered by Óscar A. Romero and translated by Claudia Castro Luna; from *Ser maestros a pesar de la violencia: Mensaje del Arzobispo de San Salvador a los maestros* (June 22, 1979).

Newspaper material in chapters 11, 13, 15, and 17 is from *Documento de la Prensa gráfica: El conflicto en El Salvador* (San Salvador: Dutriz Hermanos, 1992). Translated with permission by Claudia Castro Luna.

Printed in the United States of America

10 9 8 7 6 5 4 3 2 1

Library of Congress Cataloging-in-Publication Data

Names: Castro Luna, Claudia María, author
Title: The flowers along the way : a memoir / Claudia Castro Luna.
Description: Evanston : Curbstone Books/Northwestern University Press, 2026.
Identifiers: LCCN 2026027081 | ISBN 9798899480928 paperback | ISBN 9798899480935 ebook
Subjects: LCSH: Castro Luna, Claudia María | Castro Luna, Claudia María—Mental health | Post–traumatic stress disorder—Patients—California | Poets, American—21st century | El Salvador—History—Civil War, 1979–1992 | LCGFT: Autobiographies | Memoirs | Biographies | Personal narratives
Classification: LCC RC552.P67 C375 2026 | DDC 616.85210092—dc23/eng/20260527
LC record available at https://lccn.loc.gov/2026027081

In memory of the thousands who lost their lives
during the Salvadoran civil war

For my mother, father, and sister

And for my three children

CONTENTS

1

To Water, Water, to Spirit, Prayer

Atiquizaya, El Salvador, 1971

Months after I found myself behind the blooming sages in the front yard of my Oakland home five months pregnant and shielding my two-year old from the barrage of bullets whizzing over us, I recovered the memory of my father hoisting me up the mango tree back in Atiquizaya to watch Volcán de Fuego erupt.

When the volcano let its fiery scream rip through the heavens in September 1971, I was five years old. The day's light waned as my family prepared to witness the eruption. Papá had chosen the time knowing that the spectacle would be more visible against a darkened sky. He, an agile tree climber, rolled up his trousers and took off his shoes and socks at the foot of the regal mango tree in the center of our courtyard. Mami held my three-year old sister Camila on her hip, while my cousins Maribel, Ramoncito, Lauro, and I stood watching Papá, who used his feet to push himself up the trunk in a swift motion while reaching for the branches above his head. Soon he was swallowed up by the rich foliage. Mami shouted at him to be careful while the rest of us hooted and admired his strength and dexterity.

Once Papá reached the branches that cleared the adobe wall circling the perimeter of our house, he narrated the eruption to us with exclamations laced with marvel and profanity.

After a while he climbed down and propped up a short ladder against the generous trunk and announced that he would help anyone up who wanted to witness the historic sight. Lauro, then a high school student, readied himself. Ramoncito, a year older than me, inched closer to Mami, who still held Camila. Maribel was noncommittal and I, though nervous, said yes. Mami said she'd decide what to do after everyone else had had a chance to look. Night had embraced us now. Lauro came back down electrified with what he'd seen. Maribel, nine years old, rescinded her enthusiasm. It was my turn. I scaled the ladder and Papá helped me up to a branch high enough to clear the adobe wall. I saw the tip of the volcano's cone glowing orange and red, with lava surging over its crater and down its sloping flanks. *Could the lava reach us?* I wondered. Though Fuego smoldered menacingly, I felt Papá cinching my waist and therefore knew I was safe up in the tree's canopy. Each time the dark cone ejected its fiery breath I held mine in awe.

That day in September 1971, my family and I watched Volcán de Fuego from our home in Atiquizaya, El Salvador, a small town a mere twelve kilometers from the Guatemalan border. There are several volcanoes anchored in eastern Guatemala close to El Salvador. This means that in Atiquizaya we were never far away from a possible eruption. Volcán Chingo is the closest volcano to our town. Chingo looms large over Atiquizaya's quaint cobblestone streets—or what is left of them. My papá was born there. I spent my early childhood there. Under Chingo's gaze generations of my papá's family flourished and lived in adobe houses with red tiled roofs where iguanas sunbathed and pushed their torsos up and down at noon.

In Náhuat, "Atiquizaya" means "place of running waters." The town is located in a valley and was at one point blessed with a rich aquifer, nearby rivers, and abundant vegetation. To this day, deep green cerros surround it, and from a distance they turn a dazzling indigo. To the east of Atiquizaya the blue hills are rich with shade-grown coffee. The picturesque and twisty road up in those hills is edged with all manner of flowers—orchids, swaths of bougainvillea in hues as bright and luscious as the best silks in the world. For this, the road is known as Ruta de las Flores, or Flowers' Route. Down in the valley, Atiquizaya's umbilical cord to the rest of the world is a single road. To the north the road leads to Santa Ana, to the south it leads to Ahuachapán, a bustling city proud of its starch-white colonial church. The road southward is narrow and punctuated on either side by majestic guanacastes, their branches extending outward until their tips meet above chugging trucks, buses, and cars.

I arrived in Atiquizaya when I was a month old. Mami delivered me, her first child, at the hospital in Santa Ana, El Salvador's second largest city, where she grew up with her nine siblings and parents. Salma, one of her older sisters, was a nurse at the hospital. She knew the medical personnel well and encouraged Mami to give birth there. My Tía Salma had had a baby boy, Josué, her fifth child, nineteen days before I was born. After the birth Mami refused to return to Atiquizaya, to the adobe house she shared with my papá's people. She wanted to remain in the company of her wise and helpful sister and decided to stay at Tía Salma's house for an entire month. Papá could not hide his chagrin, so the story goes. But my Tía Salma relishes the memory and loves to tell the story of how she nursed my cousin Josué and I as if we were twins while Mami learned the intricacies of mothering a newborn.

In Atiquizaya I was perfect, the daughter of two respected teachers, Roman and Inez, the sister of Camila, the granddaughter of Camila and Ramón, the great-granddaughter of Salvador and Anita. The street I grew up on teemed with cousins, tías, and tíos. It was so that anyone marginally related to us became a cousin, an uncle, or an aunt. Set up like this our family felt, to my child self, inexhaustible, as was everyone else's family, which made living in Atiquizaya feel as if all of the town's citizens, by truth or fluke, were related to each other.

Many houses in our cobblestone-lined barrio operated as laboratories of creativity. At the top of our street, the smell of wood varnish announced Tío Julio's woodworking trade before anyone stepped into his home. A few houses down Abuela lived with her two daughters, Gina and Valeria. Every inch of their abode was devoted to their candy-making business. Next door lived Tío Samuel, his wife Doña Merced, and their seven children; their humble residence belied a large courtyard and stable where Samuel cared for the oxen with which he earned his living carrying loads. Two seamstresses, one on each side of the street, kept us dressed and fashionable. Don Galo, Doña Elba, and their three teenage daughters, Ester, Glenda, and Yuri, shared a home that was half shoe repair shop, half spice and condiment shop. Around the block a woman made and sold fresh cheese, which she dispensed on shiny squares cut from banana leaves. Traditions, craftsmanship, savvy, and beauty mated productively with necessity under the red tiled roofs of Barrio el Ángel. In the sequence of our days people came and went bringing and delivering goods, checking in, gossiping, caring for one another. We were busy and our street hummed—like a colmena—the song of life.

Atiquizaya is stored in the part of my brain where happy resides. "Happy" is another word for "not afraid." No one I knew was looking for happy when I was a child. No one I knew bothered with the concept. People visited one another's houses, told and retold the stories of the day—so-and-so's dislocated shoulder, so-and-so's passing a nursing entrance exam—recounting again and again a new birth, a recent death. The retelling made it so that we owned one another's stories and, by way of that, one another's existences.

During the Christmas season of 1971, my cousin Maribel, while pushing me on the homemade swing that then hung from the mango tree, told me in a hushed tone that Santa Claus did not exist. I jerked the swing, dug my heels into the dirt, willed a full stop.

"No, no, no," I said looking up at her, dread mowing down the joy I'd felt just seconds earlier when the warm afternoon air caressed my face.

"Sí, sí, sí," she said, working hard to hide an impish smile.

No te creo, said my stinging eyes.

"Sí. Sí." She insisted, "Your parents are the ones who put the regalos at the foot of your bed!"

With words efficient as a guillotine, she severed any filament of doubt that might have lingered inside me. To argue was futile. Santa Claus and his generous antics were a fabrication. Under our mango tree my life was irrevocably changed. A single lightning bolt is all it takes to split open our minds with a realization. Sometimes, there is time enough to prop a ladder against a tree; sometimes we stand too late in ashes.

2

Birthday Cake

Oakland, California, 2003

Twenty-two years after my family's escape from El Salvador, I was living in Oakland, California, married, the mother of a two-year old daughter, and blissfully expecting again. My pregnancy was moving along well and at a faster clip, it seemed, than my first. The smooth belly bump appeared earlier than it had with Aurora. By the fifteenth week, often over breakfast, I could feel an effervescence in my belly. Aurora was too young to notice my physical changes but soon she would start asking about my expanding midsection due to the way my hand reached for it and held it gently whenever I felt the summersaulting. By and large my life had fallen into place: I was in love with my toddler, in love with my husband, and eagerly awaiting to expand our family, only for June 19 to arrive and shatter what I had diligently worked to build in the United States.

Mild light opened the morning to announce a boundless sunny day, the kind that polishes surfaces, bodies, and actions with a veneer of optimism. In a rare moment of neighborhood serenity there were no pedestrians, bicyclists, or motorists on our otherwise busy street. In the front yard the pink cabbage roses that my father and his infallible green thumb had helped me plant on one of his visits from

El Salvador burst faultless, and white butterflies fluttered over their full heads. Across the street two cats sauntered about with sleep and dirt sticking to their fur as they moved through an overgrown front yard on their way to my neighbor Lena's front porch, where she set out food for them.

While dressing Aurora, I planned our morning's doings: a supermarket run with a visit to a toy shop to purchase a gift for the upcoming birthday party to which Aurora had been invited. Outside, we stepped hand in hand down the concrete path to the sidewalk, past twisted, overgrown lavender bushes, ground-hugging bunches of flowering pinks, and hunching wormwood in need of pruning. I loved walking with Aurora's hand in mine, my hand reaching down, her little one reaching up. The loveliness, the clasping of trust and mutuality, made me feel whole and ripe with hope for the future. Meanwhile in my womb, oblivious to roses and sunshine, and to the sweet promise of birthday cake, my five-month-old fetus swam in silky waters, enveloped in the purple night of heaven.

To our right in the garden, birds feasted on the aphids that rows of organized ants tended along the length of our birch tree, while other insects buzzed back and forth between the blooming sages and roses. To the left of us I could see that the house next to Tim's, on the corner of Aileen and Dover Streets, had an open house sign in front of it. Tim lived in a large duplex painted a warm coral with white trim. On sunny afternoons, his building radiated a soft peach, as if the hue was generated from within the walls themselves. Whereas Tim's place was cheerful, the house for sale next door to his sat dank and dirty behind a scraggly lawn. The real estate market was picking up in our neighborhood and homes in need of repair were especially selling fast.

For a second, I considered strolling over to poke around and see what type of interior improvements had been made. I kept a sharp eye out for open houses in our vicinity. I wanted to recruit friends who, like us, were starting families, to settle down in our neighborhood. This was complete wishful thinking on my part. In truth few of our friends showed interest in moving to our corner of the map. "Eclectic" is how I described our North Oakland neighborhood's housing stock, a mix of a few well-kept homes, benevolently unkempt ones, and disheveled ones with chain-link fences that kept in snarling dogs.

As I teetered between running my errands and playing real estate agent, between walking over to the open house or getting in the car, something whisked me away—something invisible like a whisper, something knowing like a friend's hand on my shoulder—and this invisible gesture convinced me to turn right instead of left, to go in the direction of our car. A succession of loud popping broke the peaceful morning spell just as I was strapping Aurora into her car seat. *Fourth of July*, I thought and pivoted in the direction of the noise expecting to see children setting off fireworks. I spotted a slender young man instead, standing next to the sign at the intersection of Aileen and Dover, aiming the barrel of a machine gun with absolute focus at something blocked from my view down Aileen Street.

At first, I thought he was trying out a new toy, maybe a special edition fireworks machine gun. But in the next deafening round I saw the fire licks and heard the hissing coming out of the mouth of the barrel. I yanked Aurora in one motion from the car seat, pulled her close, and threw us behind two large sage plants growing in front of the birch tree. Gunfire crescendoed around us. I struggled with the size of my growing belly but managed to hug Aurora, pressing her to my body.

Immobile behind the greenery, I knew leaves and spindly branches were no shield against wayward bullets. Panic built inside me the way water boils gently at first, then in violent froth. A familiar terror widened and revealed itself. My heart thumped hard against my rib cage. I wanted to stand up and scream for help. I wanted to bolt to the safety of my house. But experience told me to stay quiet and low until the shots subsided. I knew the drill. Don't move. Don't flinch. Don't draw attention.

Crouching behind the sage, I calculated which place inside the house would be the safest, where bullets would have to work the hardest to reach us. These thoughts were part of behaviors practiced back in El Salvador:

If caught on a street with no available barrier, shield yourself behind a parked car.
If you must walk during crossfire, do it flush to a wall.
Wherever you go, scout out the most sheltered place to withstand sustained gunfire.

In a snap, the morning reverted to silence.

A peek through the sage's branches confirmed what I wanted to see: The shooter was gone. I scrambled up and, with Aurora on my hip, rushed to the door. In my haste one of my sandals caught the lip of one of the river rocks I'd used to make a border around the roses and I nearly fell. When I reached the porch I fumbled in my bag for the house keys, my hands shaking, legs convulsing. I had no bones left. A screeching sound tore my attention away from the keyhole I was trying unsuccessfully to engage. From Aileen a car hung a violent left turn onto our street, shrieking and skidding. The shooter sat on the passenger side—I saw him. *Did he see me?* The lock yielded, and I thrust my body inside almost at the same time the car sped by.

Aurora had not cried or complained about the jostling, my pounding heart. I put her down only when we were nestled against the thick bookcase in the big bedroom. She searched my face in her curious toddler way; I wanted to say something pleasant and lighthearted to reassure her, maybe to reassure myself, but I was still heaving and trying to control my shakiness. The black, wall-mounted kitchen phone rang.

"Did you hear that?" It was Penn from next door. "That was right outside!"

"I was out there with Aurora." My voice trembled.

"Stay right there. I'll be right over," Penn said and hung up.

He spotted the damage as soon as he had one foot inside the house. "Your windows!"

I followed his gaze; broken glass lay strewn over the living room carpet. I must have stepped right over it and felt not a thing when I rushed in.

Penn walked around inspecting the room. "Look at this," he said, and pointed to the yellow wall pocked with bullet holes. The house still had its original lath and plaster, soft and crumbly, and the whitish plaster lay at the base of the wall from the impact of the bullets. My heart ached. Aurora's crib rested against the very spot on the other side of the wall. My throat pinched as I barely managed to articulate what I was thinking: We could have been killed inside or outside. On the other side of the opening that divided the living room from the dining room, another set of bullets had torn through a blue pad leaning against the wall. We used the pad for stretching and sometimes for Aurora's playtime.

Moments before we left the house, Aurora had been stacking her beloved colorful cups next to the mat. Penn must have seen my face struggling to make sense of my bullet-riddled living room. His arms enveloped me, and I gave up all composure. He sat me down in the kitchen, set a glass of water in front of me, and bent to my eye level.

"I don't think they are that far away," he said, "I'm going to go and drive around. See if I can find them."

"Please don't do it!" I said, alarmed. I feared he would be killed if the shooters detected him in their rearview mirror.

"I can recognize the car. I saw it from my window," he said.

"Please don't go."

"I'll just call the police. I won't do anything stupid," he said, and with a few hurried strides he was out of view. *No, no, no*, I wanted to say, *you don't go chasing after the guy with the big gun.*

No.

You hide.

No.

You run.

You run in the opposite direction for as long as you can. You get as far as you can. You go to another country if you have to. You go where no one knows you. You go where your anonymity makes you safe.

This is what I wanted to tell Penn and didn't; didn't because I could not yet grasp the long stretch behind me, the long miles I had already run.

Run. Sprint
Run. Race
Run. Dart
Run. Rush
Run. Bolt
Run. Hasten
Run. Hurry
Run. Scurry
Run. Scamper
Run. Fly
Run. Gallop
Run. Charge
Run. Scoot
Run. Shoot
Run. Hurtle
Run. Speed
Run. Zoom
Run. Zip
Run. Run. Run.

As Penn rushed out of the house, I made my way from the kitchen back to the living room. Glass shards remained scattered over the Persian rug fashioned with the tree of life motif, woven in rich reds on a yellow background. The heap of crumbled plaster was there and the bright blue, red, yellow of Aurora's stacking cups next to the blue mat had not faded in any way. I walked back to the kitchen and dialed John's cell phone number.

"John, there was a shooting in front of our house," I said, plunging into an urgent retelling of what had happened.

"Claudia, Claudia!" he said, trying to slow the hurtling words that coursed through the phone line.

"A shooting outside . . . !" I plowed on and raised my voice, trying to make him understand.

"Claudia, I am about to go into this meeting, remember?"

But, but . . .

"Please. I'll call you back as soon as I'm done. I promise."

But . . .

"Please!" He hung up on me, unable to hide his irritation.

Slowly the meeting came into focus. I'd forgotten. For weeks he had strategized about the most effective way to interest a charitable foundation in the housing advocacy nonprofit he directed. Visiting the foundation's headquarters, he was hoping to win their endorsement. I'd forgotten the care with which he had dressed that morning. He'd chosen slacks and a blue Oxford shirt, paired with black leather shoes, rather than the usual jeans and button-down under a light rain jacket he wore to pedal to work.

Three police cruisers barricaded Aileen and Dover Streets. Yellow tape sagged from post to post across the entire intersection. Bright yellow tent markers hovered over empty bullet casings on the street and sidewalk. Police, in their stark dark-blue uniforms, examined the cordoned-off area, searching intently, looking for clues from the corner of Dover and Aileen all the way to my front lawn.

Strangers and neighbors had come out, drawn by the sirens and flashing lights. They gathered in groups, talking, pointing. I ventured outside with Aurora, hungry for an explanation—and also scared. I stood at the end of our walkway, in the very spot where minutes earlier something had made me choose life. It was an eerie moment: I was physically there with my daughter's hand in mine, watching the post-shooting scene unfold, but I was absent. Gun violence could have killed me in El Salvador during the civil war my family had managed to escape, and gun violence could have killed me, my toddler, and my unborn baby in front of my house in the United States.

I made my way into the crowd.

"What are those for?" I asked a policeman standing nearby, pointing at the yellow markers.

"To help us identify the shells."

"Identify?"

"We'll count and catalogue as many shells as we can find and through that identify the gun and the person who used it. Hopefully." he said.

"What type of gun was it?" I asked, halfway expecting him to say an M-16. But I knew it could not have been. I would have never mistaken an M-16 for a toy gun.

"Some type of semi-automatic." He went on, "These kids get a hold of guns with no clue about the power they got going. With those big guns you think you are shooting in one direction, but the gun pulls you in another." He mimed holding such a gun, imitating the recoil, the unwieldy nature of the backward thrust from such a formidable weapon. I nodded.

"See here?" he asked, extending his right arm in a sweeping motion over the scene. By now people had gathered around us and huddled in to hear his take of the events.

"This guy, he thought he was shooting down Aileen, but in fact he was spraying bullets up and down Dover. These two houses over there have broken windows."

He was pointing to my house and at the fourplex on my side of the street directly across from the shooter. My legs softened like noodles once more.

"Luckily no one got hurt," the officer said and moved onto something else, away from our group.

More people arrived and chatted around the intersection. I saw a young man walking past me and wondered whether the shooters had sent a mole to inspect the damage. I was sure they had. He was their mole coming back to get a good look at me, to remember the face of the woman who watched the suspect spray bullets over our street, the woman who saw two men drive away. The perpetrators were casing me out, to identify and shoot me later. Of this I had no doubt.

I headed back into the house and soon after, I heard a knock at the door.

"Are they going to come back for me?" I asked the policeman who had come to inspect the damage and to interview me. He also wanted my signature on a statement.

"No, they are not coming back for you." He answered in what I took to be his most reassuring voice.

A photographer busied himself taking pictures of the broken windows, the glass shards on the carpet, the walls where the bullets had found their end.

"But I saw him," I clarified, "and he saw me. He saw me as I tried to run into the house . . ."

The policeman must have caught the acceleration in my voice, sensed my anxiety.

"Lady," he said firmly, boring his eyes into mine. "These gang members are not interested in whether someone sees them or not. They're not interested in passersby. They're only interested in what they're after and the people they're after. They're not interested in you. Please believe me and don't worry. They're not coming back for you." I didn't, for a second, believe him. Back in El Salvador the Death Squads came after you. They stalked you. They ambushed you. They killed you. And when they did, they left a white handprint on a nearby wall as a calling card and a warning. "You got a nice house," said the photographer, the last to leave, on his way out. *Little good it does me now,* I thought. All the care in choosing the right paint colors for each room, the deliberation over rugs, the furniture, not one thing in the house, not one person outside on the street, not John, could offer me solace.

When I scouted the intersection after the shooting, Aurora's hand in mine, I could not yet see how the morning's event had canceled years of moving forward, of chasing the American Dream. The person with the quick instincts, who knew what to do in case a shoot-out with semi-automatic weapons, was not the person I had groomed myself to be: the one who drank Earl Grey with a drop of milk and ate gorgonzola with pears when they were in season. This image of myself that I had constructed was just that: an image. A way of performing the person I wanted to be. I did not know what wilderness the shooting had thrust me into, and I could not yet conceive of the trail of crumbs that would show me the way back into myself. There was only this: Unspooling the events in front of our house was the way toward gaining some kind of understanding about my life, about the woman I had become in the US and the girl I once had been in El Salvador.

3

Mango, Mangue

Atiquizaya, El Salvador, 1972

The mango tree in our courtyard was a multifaceted creature: It provided us with luscious shade, nourished us, offered us joy, and operated as a kind of living calendar marking our days. A queen of a tree, it had a wide, lush canopy that yielded hundreds and hundreds of delicious mangoes every year. Mangoes enough for us, our neighbors, for the bats, birds and bees, and for all the insects who feasted on the fruit that fell overnight for the duration of the mango season. With such abundant harvests, no one in their right mind stooped so low as to eat a mango with a nick on its skin. Only perfect fruit would do, and to ensure this my thirty-year-old papá regularly scaled up the robust trunk to select the choicest mangoes for us to eat.

In tropical El Salvador snow exists in books and TV, but in January, when the petite white blooms of the ubiquitous mangoes open up and the wind rustles branches, petals loosen and flutter like snow flurries. By March the flowers give way to tight, small, crunchy green mangoes, or "tetelques," so named because of the astringent smack of the sap running through them. By late April we cut the first, almost-ripe fruit. Some years this happens just in time for Holy Week, adding juicy, orange mango glory to the otherwise somber commemorations.

When I was young, as the mango season wore on, we grew accustomed to the intermittent plop of fruit falling off laden branches. "If you want to touch the sky, then you must master the secret of climbing trees," Papá would say, and he deftly proved it. Barefoot, a matata across his right shoulder, he ascended and harvested unblemished fruit from the uppermost branches of our mango tree. Mami, Camila, and I shouted while he picked, pulled, and plucked until the matata bulged with fruit.

"¡Más arriba!"

"¡A la derecha!"

"¡Ese, sí!"

"¡Ese no!"

We sat in the covered corridor that faced the courtyard and devoured mangoes to our hearts' content and our stomachs' displeasure. We consumed the entire fruit, skin and flesh, letting bitter and sweet, soft and coarse, find harmony in the silks of our mouths. We ate, and the regal tree surveyed the orderly paradise beneath its branches, the figs, the miniature orange trees, the blooming hibiscus and prized roses. After feasting on the ripe fruit, Camila and I washed the seeds clear of excess pulp and turned them into dolls. We filled bowls with water and crouched to watch the seeds' fibers loosen and undulate in soft waves like the tresses of a floating mermaid. We named each seed—Maritza, Mariana, Cristina—and combed their long hair in all sorts of ways: pointy and upward, broad and sideways, and tightly along their bodies.

Camila and I enjoyed a childhood where the cadence of our days was marked by earth's song and rhythm. The walls of our house, its roof, and the tall fence that surrounded it were literally made of earth. Our house was cool even on very hot days because of its clay-tiled roof and thick adobe walls. On nights when rain fell the entire house smelled faintly of baked earth. Sometimes I played at poking and pulling bits of straw from the exposed adobe bricks of the exterior walls. Sitting in the courtyard with dirt up to our elbows, Camila and I made tortitas, packing wet earth in the tin bottle caps we collected, surrounded by the luxurious sight and smell of the roses Papá assiduously tended.

Camila was quick and lithe, with obsidian eyes that burned and sparkled and brightened her face like a small sun no matter the time of day. She acquired new words with alacrity, especially bad ones, and deployed them with searing accuracy. In that respect she took after our abuela, whose namesake she was. The regal older woman and the charming granddaughter dueled life under the name's umbrella, heirs of a long line of fierce and resolute female ancestors. Camila had a birthmark just above her right lip that accentuated her face in a most pleasing way whenever she smiled, prompting strangers upon meeting her for the first time to ask, "¿Me lo regalas?" She was used to the question and was adept at letting folks who asked down easy. No, she was not about to give away her beloved birthmark.

Camila didn't walk around with her head in the clouds or dwell too long on things like I did. The younger sister, she was smaller in stature, but in many ways, she was my protector. Pity the kid who dared slight me in any way, because my sister's wrath would soon follow—a kind of pounding, torrential rain. It was not pleasant. I had been plenty deluged by her tongue's unleashing. Where Camila was sun, I was moon, and the two of us knew how to circumnavigate the universe of our household. We marked the sky, stirred the earth, and each day complemented each other.

On hot afternoons, relishing the quiet siesta hour and taking advantage of the coolness of the living room, Papá played his classical music records and burrowed, deeply, into one of his many books. Once the slow—and, to me, mournful—music filled the living room, the air became thick and sticky like masa for tortillas. The music spilled into the corridor and crossed the courtyard, spreading faint tendrils around the trunks of all the trees that thrived in our backyard. I bolted as far away from the record player as I could, through the courtyard, past the vegetable garden and the fruiting trees, all the way to the tapial—the back adobe wall—where the music had the hardest time reaching me.

At that hour the sun's wrath cut equally through leaf and stone; only iguanas and lizards were appreciative denizens. They bowed their reptilian heads up and down and curtsied incessantly with their short legs. At the back of the house, I shared my time with the chirimoyas, jocotes, aguacates, guayabas, huddled under their green awnings. I joined the realm of the zompopos, who knew how to devour leaves and pinch skin. Oh, how these ants with their sharp, maxillary prowess frustrated Papá by eating up his vegetables and destroying his roses. In single file they marched one-two-three, one behind the other, carrying on their backs leaf chunks several times bigger than themselves. I prodded the zompopos with sticks, threw leaf bits at them, pursued them to their nests, and then poked, poked, poked until they ran crazily around, spilling over one another, a fierce, snapping, red chaos, ay, ay, ay, each bite pinching like lightning through my skin.

Papá shared his love freely only with two things: his books and his garden. He did not need companions for these tasks. He lived them alone. Sometimes I scooted up to him while he was busily pruning, transplanting, or grafting in his rose garden. At those moments his narrow face was focused and relaxed and smiles were easy to come by. In the company of plants Papá was animated; plants lent him a kind of energy, a boost that was not evident in most other situations. His interest in plants and in the natural world was why he would eventually pursue a degree in biology at the Universidad de El Salvador. I liked watching his dirt-caked fingers maneuver his gardening knife, tear a piece from an old shirt, and tie the long cloth piece securely around a new graft. I liked the way his slender body felt loose and the way his voice was generous and soft in those moments. I wished more than anything that by being close to him, some of the love he poured into his plants would spill onto me.

Whereas my father was taciturn and melancholic, my mother was gregarious and vivacious. For him classical music was great, but for her Celia Cruz was better. The sixth child of a family of ten, Mami relished company and thrived in group settings. She was prone to dancing when a song she liked came on the radio. At Christmas time, with her sisters and brothers, nieces and nephews, the dancing went on for hours. Papá joined her on these occasions and my heart swelled watching them holding each other close, their bodies keeping rhythm. They were happy together and I was happy to be their daughter.

Mami, a year younger than Papá, arrived in Atiquizaya after she married him, but she never quite jived with the small town's simpler way of life. Adobe walls, the lack of potable water, the absence of a sewage system, the cobblestone streets so unfriendly to heels, all this grated on her. Mami did not appreciate the church's hold on people and folk's adherence to what she called old beliefs and superstitions. Her wish had always been to return to the busier rhythms of the city of Santa Ana, where her own mother lived with Tía Salma.

Mami was a modern woman, too modern for the God-fearing ways of Atiquizaya. She favored above-the-knee A-line dresses over the below-the-knee cut most women in town wore. She preferred heels when everyone else walked in flat slip-on shoes or sandals. When the times changed and wide-legged jeans, macramé, and thick-soled huaraches became fashionable, she switched her wardrobe accordingly. She scoffed at the ancient ways that prevailed in Atiquizaya: babies wearing ojo de venado bracelets to ward off the evil eye, visiting sobadoras—women healers—to expunge "aire" instead of taking a painkiller. She read *Vanidades* and *Buenhogar*, fashion and style magazines unheard of in our barrio. Whenever she prepared one of the suggested recipes, if she was happy with the results, she clipped and pasted it in a special journal she kept. Flipping through the pages of her magazines, I'd want her to follow the suggestions offered: paint walls that way, sew curtains this way, macramé such and such. I'd get excited about possible embellishments to our house and then I'd realize that none of the suggestions applied to us; no one I knew lived or ate as depicted in these magazines. The women I knew did not wear trousers and often wore an apron with wide pockets over their dresses. People in the neighborhood slaughtered chickens in their backyards and maybe a piglet for special occasions; back then no one I knew bought meat from a supermarket shelf.

When I lived in Atiquizaya washing was done entirely by hand, and in some houses, ironing was still a matter of heating an actual iron with hot burning coals. Oxen pulling carts shared the road with cars and buses around town. Nothing in the pages of any magazine I came across when I was a child ever reflected the reality of our lives. Things for us were as they were. Imperfect. We clustered around the routines that held our lives together and assumed that our relationships with one another would continue as they always had.

The togetherness of our days entwined with our joys, our frustrations, our hopes, and our lack. There was the lack of potable water, the sight of men wasted on cheap rum, wasting in their joblessness, the stink of shit and garbage in the gutters, the gutters in men's eyes. Street dogs scratched behind their ears as their bellies shrunk with thirst and hunger, and flies, ever insistent, swooped down on our plates even as we ate. But the mountains singing in perfect indigo were on our side. Rain for the corn and bean harvests came punctually each May, and the shortcuts and networks of assistance we cobbled up nourished and sustained us.

So much of I what know about the world, the seen and unseen of it, its mystery and spiritual dimension, comes from those early days in Atiquizaya. My abuela, Papá's mother, was and remains my supreme teacher. As soon as I was of age, which is to say, as soon as I could speak and walk, she took me under her wing and taught me the things she thought I needed to carry to navigate life. She taught me how to cross myself. "Por la señal de la Santa Cruz . . ." she said, and I quickly scrambled after her, repeating her words and clumsily copying her hand making the sign of the cross. She helped me along, placing my thumb over my index finger to form a cross, and guided me, pausing first over my forehead, then over my cheeks, then to navel and shoulders, finishing on my lips. "Kiss the cross," she said. And I did. I kissed it and uttered a reverent, "Amen."

My abuela was kind to me, her first grandchild, but patience was not one of her virtues. By necessity she was a woman of swift action. Widowed in her early twenties, her emotional repertoire skewed toward determination, grit, and an irascible temper. In a fraction of a second, she could go from laughing heartily to reaching perilous levels of anger. One of her searing and creatively strung list of insults could flat out shake off all the leaves of a mango tree, leaving birds cowering atop bare branches. Lucky for me, she loved me, her oldest grandchild, and she worked hard to pass along the array of recipes, amulets, prayers, and rituals known to her so that I may live a long and fruitful life under the winning patronage of all the saints and angels in heaven.

Acceptance of mystery was a cornerstone of my abuela's beliefs. Mystery connected her to something bigger, brighter, kinder than the material circumstances under which she lived. Our senses could only take us so far—reality could not be gauged by perceived evidence alone. Just because you couldn't see something, didn't mean it was not real. For her, the unseen world ordered and balanced the visible one. My abuela's conviction that mystery and magic existed was sewn into her marrow. The years I spent at her side in the open-air kitchen where she prepared candies for a living insured that it was sewn into mine.

Abuela's certainty about the unseen world is why I believed in spirits such as el Cipitío and la Siguanaba. Cipitío liked to visit houses at night to eat the ashes from the poyos, the wood and clay stoves over which the comal to make tortillas was placed. It was said that Cipitío liked to nap in quiet corners under his large conical straw hat—his only clothing item. Every kid I knew, including Camila and I, checked the poyos first thing in the morning in hopes of finding Cipitío's backward-facing footprints in the ashes. Cipitío was an eternal child, a duende, living freely among the trees, like ghosts and birds. Cipitío was one of several magical and ancient beings who lived among us, sure as the sun shone above our heads.

Every now and then, Abuela brought Camila and me toys she picked up at the Chalchuapa market, where she had a stall from which she sold her candies and confections. She gifted us toy-sized clay pots, dishes, and cups, doll furniture strung with tule, hand-stitched clothing, children's versions of adult shopping bags and baskets. All the toys she brought us bore the stamp of handmade things: slightly irregular and slightly imperfect and, for those reasons, all the more lovely. These were the people's toys, and if she had ever any as a child, they must have looked not much different than the ones she regaled us with.

For all her bluster and impetuousness Abuela also sought calmness and grace. She taught me that to make oneself whole, one needed to honor spirit and spend time in silence and contemplation. For her this space was found in the sanctuary of the church, or in front of the small altar she kept in her room with the images of the Sacred Heart of Jesus and of Saint Jude flanked with a clump of rue, a candle, and a container filled with water. She took me to mass with her whenever she could. One year, she took me on pilgrimage to Guatemala to visit el Cristo Negro de Antigua.

For my part, I relished Abuela's company, her sayings, her superstitions and, above all, her spiritual teachings. I wished nothing more ardently than to make my Holy Communion. I yearned to have a picture of myself in a long white dress, a diadem of sparkling beads resting on my head and gloved hands holding a candle like my friends and cousins had in their living rooms. For me the ceremony involved in making a Primera Comunión was a kind of initiation. The world of ritual, of reverence, the mystery of the unknown, the existence of God, being in a dark, quiet space with traces of incense was pure magic to me. The realm of spirit pulled me hard. My abuela venerated this unseen realm, she knew its traditions, she practiced them without reservation, and she welcomed me into her world. She shared her life with me. She shared all of her with me, and this has made all the difference.

To the naked eye of my child self the civil war which was to explode in less than a decade was nowhere visible, but its spores were slowly and silently finding purchase in the soil under our feet. I don't think anyone at the time could yet point a finger at it. But explode it did, and when it came it stomped and assailed cities and countryside equally, it wounded young and old, it killed rich and poor; its nefarious hand left nothing untouched.

Each night before she went to sleep, Abuela left a glass of water next to her bed and urged me to do the same. "Siempre deja un vaso de agua al lado de tu cama," she'd say. Our souls roam free at night, she explained, and the filled glass assures they will not go thirsty in the time of darkness. The glass and its liquid also served as a beacon, a signpost, for a soul to find its respective body after its nightly meander. She spoke these things with absolute certainty, and her stories simultaneously fascinated and terrified me. I trembled imagining my soul lost, out in the world, unable to find its way back into my body, which in a way is precisely what happened when the war came.

4

Say Peace

Oakland, California, 2003

By the time John arrived home the yellow tape had been taken down and discarded, the bullet tents folded and put away, the crowds dispersed, and the police dispatched to other calls and crimes.

"I'm so sorry," he said and held me for a long time while we stood in our kitchen. I could tell by the way he held me that he had underestimated the situation I'd tried to convey over the phone. We sat down facing each other at the kitchen table, the way we did at breakfast and in the evening. Behind us in the living room, windowpane shards and bullet holes in walls told of our sudden anything-but-normal situation. Aurora climbed onto John's lap and with a deep inhale I told him everything.

My body was too large, yet not large enough for the retelling. I spoke but could not find my footing. Who was speaking? The girl back in El Salvador? A young mom who almost lost her child to bullets? A woman self-editing what she should feel at a time like this? When the tears rolled, whose tears were they? I ran down corridors inside my mind, gasping, knocking on doors, hoping that behind one of them I'd find my true self, who would know how to respond to these feelings. John held my hands and told me again and again how sorry he was that this had happened. After a while he stood up to check out the damage. I followed him into the living room but stopped at the shattered window and watched him walk to the corner of Aileen and Dover. He stood in front of the corner building, surveying the scene. Two windows on the ground floor apartment facing Dover Street had taken bullets. He strolled up and down our sidewalk, staring at our house, then again back to the intersection.

"The police missed some bullets," he said, coming back straight into the kitchen, "I spotted two holes on the side gate and a few below the windows in front of the house."

"Where do you think those bullets landed?" I asked.

"Probably stuck in the vinyl siding. Gone through into the crawl space, maybe."

"Two shots hit the gate?" I asked, feeling the dread of the shooting run through me again. "Aurora and I were right in front of it!"

"If you had not bent down . . ." He didn't need to finish the sentence.

"We need to leave," I blurted. "They saw me. They will come back for me. I just know it!"

"I don't know that they'll do that," John said. "They're probably on the run as we speak—trying to get as far away from Oakland as possible."

I was not buying any of it. What did he know about people with automatic rifles?

"We really should be thinking about how to replace those windows," he went on, poking into the refrigerator, looking for a snack. "They can't stay like that for much longer."

He joined me at the kitchen table with one of the fujis we'd bought on our last run to Berkeley Bowl and I stared him down. I was not letting go. I feared the men would be merciless with me.

"And where would we go anyhow?" he asked, resigned to my bullheadedness.

I knew John did not understand my need to leave the house, but taking stock of the calamitous state of my nerves, he was at least willing to go along with me. I ran through our friends' names and we both agreed that our best bet was Liam. He was one of John's closest friends in the Bay Area. He rented a ground floor apartment in North Berkeley next to a sweet pocket-sized park. It would be easier for him to accommodate us—he could crash at his girlfriend's in San Francisco. To my relief Liam not only agreed to the overnight stay but made his place available to us for a few days.

I packed hastily. Enough diapers and outfits for Aurora, food for our pug dog, and a thoughtless array of clothes thrown in an overnight bag for me. Poor Toby; in my haste to get into the house and in my anxious state, I had hardly noticed him. He, too, must have been scared. It offered me some solace that his basket, his safe space, was in a corner of the dining room, next to the kitchen and away from the line of fire.

In less than an hour we were on our way to Liam's small apartment. He lived at the back of a stately home. The path to his place ran the length of the two-story house; we walked brushing against tall mallows on one side and camellias on the other. The house shaded the mallows, and they had developed gangly branches that reached upward in search of light. The shade and intimacy they created along the path echoed the lush patios of El Salvador. The row of mallows arched, forming a green tunnel, and their white flowers became to me like stars against a hopeful firmament.

We huddled at Liam's for two days and I clung to every minute, holding on to the safety his verdant home offered. The kitchen opened to a large rustic deck surrounded by small-leaved shrubs, vines, and the soft-branched mallows. Just beyond, on the other side of the natural fence provided by the shrubs, was the small park, which was seldom used. The setting was the perfect antidote for my unsettled nerves. Sitting on the deck, I watched Aurora go about her toddler business and I grew convinced that what we needed to do was move away to a tranquil place, similar to this one, miles away from our house.

The cottage on Dover Street we had put so much love and effort into had, in a few hours, become a liability. Creativity, diligence, and patience had transformed it from a run-down, sticky, stinky mess into a comfortable home. One of its best attributes was its affordability. But at that moment the benefits of owning our house, the comfort, the garden, were unimportant. I was willing to give it all up on the spot. The unchewed cud of memories from my last days in El Salvador swirled in the pit of my stomach.

I knew that running away from danger was what my family had done to stay alive. Running was familiar to me. Running was exactly what I now wanted to do. Run away and start up in a new place that had no trace of the shooting, no trace of this fear that brewed and bubbled inside me. On some level, I sensed that I was overreacting. The police and everyone else insisted that the men were not going to return to the neighborhood. Quite the contrary, everyone said—they were probably on the run and as far from the corner of Aileen and Dover Streets as they could manage. A glimmer of understanding told me I was conflating the contours of two fears: the one I had lived days earlier and the one I had buried decades before.

In the weeks following our return to Dover Street, I strived to return to my old routines, but something was amiss, and I behaved erratically. At first, I considered these episodes one-time occurrences, but the more they happened, the more I came to realize they were part of a pattern rather than single stitches. I read banal events as harbingers of doom. My brain turned any young man walking in front of our house who saw me at the window into a spy sent to case me out, to tally out my daily routine and set up an ambush. It turned a woman with her small dog stopping to admire my roses into an informant. A gust of wind tussling the foliage of the birch tree in front of the house became a sign from the ghost who saved me the morning of the shooting. White butterflies above the sages announced an impending death. I now saw things through a filter of fear and anxiety, changing the hue and dimension of everything around me.

While we were away at Liam's, John had the windows replaced. I was thankful for his diligence, but these kinds of concerns were exactly the type of troubles I no longer wanted to deal with. I did not want to live in a neighborhood where car windows were often smashed, where Christmas lights hanging on a porch were subject to theft, or where bullets shattered living room windows.

"You shouldn't worry so much," Edith said, standing in the kitchen with a mug of coffee.

I worked part-time; Edith took care of Aurora on my workdays. She also came from El Salvador, but she'd left the country years before the war. "Niña," she went on, "things like this can happen anytime, in any neighborhood. Don't think that moving to a different neighborhood will save you from this type of violence." She looked at me with her soft dark eyes. "Ay, Edith, si solo fuera verdad," I said, not knowing whether what she said was true.

5

Election Time

Atiquizaya, El Salvador, 1972

The frontrunners of the presidential election were a civilian and a military man: José Napoleón Duarte and Coronel Arturo Armando Molina. Duarte represented the UNO (Unión Nacional Opositora) and Molina the PCN (Partido de Conciliación Nacional). Molina's party was the establishment party, their eponymous symbol a white-and-blue flag with a triangle containing two shaking hands. Duarte's party was a center left coalition and their symbol was a fish, a volcano, and a tecomate—a gourd—to convey that theirs was a fight for the people, for el pueblo. I reacted strongly to the candidates. Duarte appeared like a friendly person, always neatly dressed, with hair starched to one side so perfectly that it looked like a dog had licked it into place. Molina, on the contrary—with his thick mustache, pursed eyebrows, and military uniform—looked scary, somewhere between a toad and a mean uncle. Like a man who was all too quick to slip off his belt and lash out for the smallest infraction.

The popular, as opposed to the official, UNO party slogan was "Con Duarte y aunque no me harte"—With Duarte even if I don't eat—which was a direct reference to the state in which many lived.

There were men and women in Atiquizaya walking over cobblestone streets shoeless or clad in sandals fashioned out of rubber tires and leather strips. I had friends at school whose worn-out uniforms and frayed shoes spoke of their families' financial struggles. There were barefoot children in the area as well, and they did not make it to school at all.

As election day neared, the contest became impossible to ignore. Radio and newspapers ran campaign ads, leaflets appeared on lampposts and on the broad walls of corner houses.

Airplanes flew low overhead and dropped thousands of party propaganda leaflets. Whenever we heard an airplane, we children scrambled to the middle of the street, jumping and shouting "¡Tire papeles, tire papeles!"—Throw us leaflets, throw us leaflets!—gleefully and at the top of our lungs. If we had not long ago agreed that our play money consisted of chips from discarded porcelain plates and cups, the leaflets would have made excellent play currency.

Every afternoon, a parade of merchants walked through the town's streets peddling homemade goods such as cheese, sweet breads, tamalitos, garden vegetables, or fruit from their backyard trees. Each person had developed a particular pitch or singsong way of announcing their goods:

"¡Coyoles en miel, Coyoles en miiiiiiiiiieeeeeeeeel!"

"¡Queso fresco, queso fresco, quesito fresco!"

"¡Barquillos, barrrrquillos, barrrrquillos!"

One such afternoon I witnessed Mami get into a verbal spat with a man selling guavas. Mami stood on the sidewalk, which was about a good two feet above the street below. She wore her melon-colored robe because it was the siesta hour, and she had been napping when she heard the man calling out to advertise the guavas. He stood on the cobblestones below and laid his wide basket on the sidewalk, offering her the chance to inspect his fruit. Between selecting guavas and making small talk, they landed on the election. The man said he was voting for Coronel Molina. Surprised, Mami leaned forward and—in a voice laced with frustration and condescension, even—told him why he shouldn't do that.

"No señor, ¿no ve que el PCN solo protege a los ricos?" she said. Don't you see that the PCN is interested only in protecting the wealthy? She built her argument using an earnest tone.

"No, es que ellos nos van a ayudar señor, ellos dicen que van a cambiar las cosas," he said, full of conviction. They will change things for sure.

He argued his point. She argued hers. I sat on the step that led up to our front door and watched. Her frustration crept out in sharper and sharper words; his spread over his weathered face, protected by a wide-brimmed straw hat. He was stubborn and she lost composure. More and more it looked like she wanted to abandon her persuasive skills and pick a fight. They glared at each other across their divide. Frustrated, he took his basket off the sidewalk—and with it, the chance of making a sale—and walked away in a huff. Incensed, Mami spun around, her hand still holding the two sides of her house robe together, and marched back into our house.

It was not difficult, even at my age, to be aware of the gross inequities under which we lived. My parents spoke of the injustices in El Salvador, they talked with each other about the things they witnessed in the schools where they taught, and because they were involved in the teacher's union—Asociación Nacional de Educadores Salvadoreños (ANDES)—they also spoke of how the country's political representatives did not favor policies to improve the lives of poor and working people. I remember Mami sharing that she had found a child staring at a slender white worm crawling on her desk. When Mami asked where it had come from, the child pointed to her mouth. Intestinal parasites were a huge health concern back when I was in elementary school, before health care became what it is today. I knew that children with distended stomachs were most likely infected with parasites. Nothing terrified me more than the thought of ingesting food or drinking well water tainted with the eggs of parasitic worms.

As a child I noticed that many children my age did not have the kinds of toys, clothes, shoes, and other general things that I took for granted. I could see that people in our barrio and in our own extended family struggled financially. Tío Samuel's entire family of seven kids subsisted on the earnings he made hauling goods in his ox cart. The two oldest sons did not pursue schooling beyond basic education and joined apprenticeships instead. Lauro was the first in their family to become a teacher, following in his tío's—my papá's—footsteps.

Of all of Tío Samuel's children, I was closest to Lauro and Cornelia. Lauro was kind, playful, and never tired of joining troops of neighborhood kids in our street games. He jumped right into béisbol stints, into chase mayhems, and joined hide-and-seek games without reservation. He even linked hands with us when we circled round and round singing nursery rhymes at the top of our lungs. Cornelia was two years older than me. I admired her and tried to imitate her in any way I could. We were inseparable, except early in the morning when I walked to school with Papá—but come afternoon we walked side by side back from school for our midday meal and returned together for the rest of our school day. Purposely we took the long way back from school alongside the train tracks and counted the steps we could walk without falling off the rails. We dared each other, laughed together, told each other our ultimate secrets. When, on a rainy day, she showed up at our door with her notebooks inside a plastic bag, I quickly emptied my two-buckled school bag onto my bed and placed my pencils and notebooks in a plastic bag to match her.

But for all that we shared Cornelia and I also lived vastly different lives. Whereas I wore polished black shoes to school, she wore sandals. Whereas my parents could afford someone to help out in the household with the cooking and washing, her entire family worked the length of the annual school break from dawn to dusk harvesting coffee to contribute to the household's budget. The national school calendar was strategically scheduled to coincide with the peak of the coffee harvest and entire families went up into the hills to take advantage of the work.

Several years later, when I was older and our family had moved to Santa Ana, I begged my parents to let me return to Abuela's house in Atiquizaya to join Cornelia and Lauro's family in the harvest. Mami was uneasy with the idea but acquiesced. I packed several shorts thinking that I needed the flexibility and comfort they afforded to walk, bend, sit, run, and whatever else I imagined I would encounter up in the hills where shade-grown coffee fincas were located. On the first day Abuela woke me up at 4:30 A.M., and by 5:00 A.M. I was trailing behind Cornelia's family, hiking up the steep hills around Atiquizaya to the fincas—the coffee plantations. Once there, a foreman, a caporal, assigned each family or group of people a row of trees to harvest. To my eye these rows appeared interminable. Before we set to work, Cornelia and Lauro's family made a bonfire and Doña Merced, their mother, placed several ripe plantains against the coals.

She heated tortillas as well. We ate squatting or sitting around the fire. My shorts, which left my legs exposed and vulnerable to dirt and scratches, were sorely out of place in the rough terrain. Doña Merced and my cousins smartly outfitted themselves with men's trousers under their skirts to protect their limbs.

Once refreshed and with food in our bellies, we set to work. The coffee plants were tall and laden with clusters of jewel-red berries. When ripe, the berries are sticky and emit a vile, cloying sweetness. Each berry had to be picked by hand. The sticky juice, to which dirt and dust stubbornly clung, soon coated our fingers and palms. Inevitably, green berries, or not-quite-ripe ones, fell into the baskets we carried around our waists, but we received full payment only for the fully ripe red ones. For me the task of selecting only the ripe berries from tightly packed bunches was slow going. I became clear to me that a pair of laboring adults could not possibly work fast enough to earn a living. This is why entire families went up to the hills during harvest season.

Not long into the workday, I stepped into a pile of leaves at the foot of a shady tree to pee and in seconds I had a swirl of red ants pinching their way up my legs. At the end of that first day, bug bites and scratches from the vegetation I had stumbled against covered my legs. To make things worse, as the first day wore on, I became familiar with the fuzzy caramel-colored caterpillars who linger on branches and under the dark coffee tree leaves and whose fur burns the skin on contact. The labor exhausted me so much I passed on dinner and crawled into bed each of the days I worked. On the second and third days I reluctantly heeded Abuela's wake-up call. I joined Cornelia's family sleepy and hungry. When we came down the hills on the third day, Mami was waiting for me at Abuela's house. I could not believe my luck. She was worried and had come to check in on me. It was a good thing, because I was running up a fever. Cornelia and her siblings did not have the choice to quit after three days. If they did not spend their entire school break up in the fincas harvesting coffee, then there would be not enough money in the household budget to afford the mandated school uniforms and supplies.

When the day for the presidential election arrived, Papá worked at a local polling station. Doña María watched over Camila and me while she prepared my papá's almuerzo, and together we walked down our cobblestone street to deliver the food. The polling station was near a park. The venerable ceibas, their wide trunks painted white, offered shade to street vendors and to all who waited to board regional buses going to Santa Ana or Ahuachapán. We found him sitting with other poll workers behind long tables, checking identity papers against voter rolls. Cédulas were the official identification document. They resembled a very small passport and the adults I knew never left home without them. After a poll worker confirmed a person's identity, they handed over a ballot but held on to their cédula. The person voted behind a screen to protect their privacy, slipped the ballot into an urn, and returned to the poll worker to retrieve their cédula. At this point each voter was asked to dip a finger in a small tub containing indelible ink which stained said finger purple. Each person who voted carried the mark of their vote on their body, thus preventing them from slipping into another polling station to vote again.

It was obvious by the wide smile on his face when he greeted us that Papá was pleased with the turnout. He stayed put until the polls closed in the evening, buoyed by the hope of a better future and a political process that appeared to be working with a fair, peaceful election. That same evening, radio reports indicated that Duarte was in the lead, just as expected. By morning, the government had imposed a media blackout on election results. The blockade lasted three days, at the end of which revised figures placed Molina and Duarte in a tie. The fraud was obvious to everyone. The National Assembly—controlled by the PCN—made the ultimate decision, giving Molina and his party the win. Duarte ended up in exile in Venezuela.

The UNO's unofficial election slogan was "Con Duarte y aunque no me harte." It had two parts: Duarte and hunger. Now that Duarte was no more, only the hunger remained. Poverty accompanied us everywhere we went, its violence evident in all facets of life. Everywhere I looked, it stared back at me, from the barefoot children I saw in Atiquizaya to the lack of infrastructure in our homes: no sewage, no potable water.

San Salvador is also known as el Valle de la Hamacas, or the Valley of Hammocks, because the city is nestled in a volcanic valley that is susceptible to periodic seismic activity, which turns it into a kind of swaying hammock. Pedro de Alvarado lives in the history books as the man who conquered El Salvador, the one who superimposed

Christian names onto our existing place nomenclatures. Kuskatan became El Salvador. I grew up swinging back and forth between all of Kuskatan's faults: seismic, geological, historical, political, cultural, economic. We swing to this day in the half-moons of our hamacas and continue to share with one another the best of what we have—even if we think we have nothing. But we have plenty, which is to say ourselves, our stories, our courage, our prayers, our resilience, and our laughter.

Duarte's advantage going into the election was palpable and the early results the evening of the election pointed to him as the eventual winner; his defeat was more than his defeat. It showed citizens, like my parents, that none of their work to run a fair campaign, to get out the vote, and to have peaceful and orderly elections mattered. Molina's manufactured win signaled that the wealthy and the military had no interest in democracy; their interest lay in holding on to their power to exploit land and to steer commerce and industry for their enrichment no matter what. It also portended the suppression of any dissent even if the cost was civilians' lives. I've asked myself many times when, at which point, did I go from living a happy childhood to treading through a war zone? To my understanding, the great sham of the 1972 election was the spark that led to the country's undoing.

6

Nothing Blue

Oakland, California, 2003

After the morning of June 19, I never drove, nor walked, past the corner of Aileen and Dover. Every time I looked at the stop sign for more than a few seconds, the young man with the black cap materialized, a machine gun in his grip. Inside the house, I wandered compulsively to the front windows to ensure nothing out of the ordinary was happening on the street. I checked, double-checked, and triple-checked that the front door lock was fully engaged. I took extreme caution when getting Aurora in and out of her car seat. Any unexpected sound set my body on extreme alert, my heart racing, and my hands sweating. I habitually placed my hand protectively over my taut belly to ensure that my baby was still thriving in her briny bubble.

Early one morning, while walking to a meeting at the Museum of Children's Art, where I managed the education programs, I spotted two figures a few blocks away approaching me on the same side of the street. The streets of Old Oakland were just waking up; fog clung with barnacle tenacity to cement and brick. I was running late for my meeting and taking long strides to gobble up the blocks from my car to the office. Upon seeing the men's figures, I went into panic mode and accelerated my pace. I looked around the street, spotted a few parked cars—just in case I needed to crouch behind one—and switched sides of the street. I could feel my neck and back knotting with tension, my defense mechanisms sounding their highest alert. At the same time, I understood that I was a stranger to those men, who most likely couldn't care less about me, whether I was afraid of them, with child or not, friend or foe. Their lives had nothing to do with mine. They probably didn't even register me as they walked on past, lost in their conversation. These heightened levels of awareness and bodily reactions happened simultaneously and frequently. They were intrusive, leaving me exhausted and confused. My body and mind reacted differently to the same events. The mind said there is nothing to worry about. The body meanwhile activated, sweated, and failed to register the message.

Another day, driving back from Aurora's preschool, I spotted a young man waiting for a bus. He walked over to the curb and craned his neck to see if the bus was coming. As I rolled on closer to where he was standing, his head moved in my direction. He looked straight at me. One of his hands was behind his back and in the next second, I expected him to swing his arm forward and point a gun in my direction. I sunk the gas pedal and flew past the bus stop. The car screeched as I veered right onto the next available street. With a heave the car came to a full stop, my whole body shaking, my skin covered in a sticky sweat.

Weeks after the shooting, every time I saw a young man who resembled the shooter, I fell into the same fear-based trap. These incidents all started and ended the same way: After the initial shock subsided, I recognized that my reaction was an unconscious reliving of the shooting in front of the house. No matter where my daily activities took me, a ghost of me remained in the house in the aftermath of the shooting, astonished at the window shards on the yellow carpet and at the pool of crushed plaster stacked next to the baseboard. There was me and a ghost of me, but having that understanding did not deter, nor lessen, my reactions to triggering events. I overreacted each and every time. It was like having an autoimmune disorder. Reliving the shooting whenever I saw a person who faintly resembled the shooter brought on war memories, which prompted my paranoid feelings about being ambushed and assassinated, which then birthed a self-loathing for overreacting. It was debilitating. I felt confused. I did not like myself. I became depressed.

One day, Jane, the new neighbor on the block, knocked on my door. She'd brought with her a small bouquet she'd hand-snipped from her front garden.

"I want to tell you how sorry I am that this happened to you," she said, sitting at the kitchen table holding a cup of tea.

"Thank you," I said looking into her soft face.

I ventured out on a limb and told her that the situation had reminded me of living in El Salvador during the civil war. Jane listened politely. She offered kind sympathy, but it was clear she had no clue what war I was talking about. She reached over anyway and rested one of her hands on top of mine when I welled up with emotion. *Who cares about what happened to me when I was fourteen years-old?* I thought.

Hadn't I been given a chance to forget?

More and more often John told me in his gentle way that working with a therapist would help me sort through what happened in front of our house. My response was abrasive at best and always the same: "And what is therapy really going to do? I'm not going to sit there and spill my guts to a stranger. Not doing it." But the day I told him about the incident with the youth at the bus stop—how panic overtook me as I sped down the busy boulevard, how the car tires screeched as I forced an abrupt right-hand turn, how I jerked to a stop, sobbing at my own madness, all while Aurora was in the back seat—was the day he lost his gentle tone.

"I've told you a hundred times: You need to see a therapist!" he said, plunking down the beer he was drinking onto the kitchen table. A half hour earlier he had parked his bicycle in the backyard. I'd heard him open the front gate from my spot chopping onions at the kitchen counter. "Please make an appointment tomorrow. You can get into an accident trying to outrun people who clearly are not after you. Just to think you had Aurora with you!" he said, shaking his head.

"I don't need a therapist," I said, raising my voice. "We need to move away from this house to a different neighborhood where things like this don't happen. That's what we need!" I said, and turned away from him to finish my dinner prep.

"Claudia, you know the housing market is crazy right now. We can sell the house, but where could we afford to live in this city?" He took a sip from his beer, then extended his arms out to Aurora who was nearby stacking dolls on a toy baby carrier while Toby watched her from a corner in the kitchen. Aurora was too focused on her game to accept John's invitation. "I really think what you need is professional help," he said and his eyes trailed off to the garden, through the French door we had installed, where foxgloves waved their magenta spears.

"John, we can find something if we look hard enough," I said, ignoring the part about my mental health and focusing instead on the tangible issue of where to live. "How about if we enlist a real estate agent?"

I knew I'd tread on dangerous ground with the mention of a real estate agent. He despised them for the speculative bidding they encouraged, which was in full display again as housing prices in the Bay Area escalated. The move backfired, just as I had suspected.

"Please, call the therapist tomorrow," he said. And it was a kind of order.

I knew he was right. I was lost. I needed help.

7

Borrón y Cuenta Nueva

From Atiquizaya to Santa Ana, El Salvador, 1974

On the grassy knoll at the top of our cobblestone street, I told Cornelia we were leaving.

"¿Qué?" she said. "¿Se van lejos?"

"No tan lejos," I said trying to soften the blow. "Santa Ana is not that far away, hombre, ¡y mi abuela Emérita vive allá!"

"¿Y qué tiene?" she responded, shrugging her shoulders. She asked what my mother's mother had to do with us moving to Santa Ana.

We spoke quickly, going back and forth, imagining how our separation might play out. What things would irrevocably have to change; what things might be salvaged. Our words jumped out of our mouths, knocked about the cobblestones, and rolled down the street the way our ball did when we played béisbol after school. We could still see each other, I wanted to say. But we both knew that unless I came to Atiquizaya, chances were less than slim that she would ever visit me.

"¿Van a tener inodoros blancos?" she asked with a hint of resignation.

"¡Sí!" I said with an air of self-importance. Yes. Our new house had indoor plumbing. I would use a flushing toilet and shower indoors for the first time in my life.

"Qué bonito," she said, then the eyes inside her eyes looked past me. We were now ambling downhill toward our respective houses, and dinner. The evening light tinged the façades of our homes mellow watermelon shades.

"Ya pronto me vas a contar que se mudan a San Salvador y después a los Estados Unidos," Cornelia said, her plastic sandals conforming to the backs of the cobblestones. I found her idea that we would eventually move to San Salvador, and one day even to the US, preposterous and outlandish. I knew only one thing about los Estados Unidos. I knew there was a city named Chicago. My Tía Valeria shared that with me one evening while she was chopping a basketful of coconut strips for the day's conservas. Chicago. That is what we called a Ferris wheel: la Chicago. Who would name a city after an amusement ride? It took me a while to get over my disbelief in between bouts of laughter. Tía Valeria put the knife down on the chopping block balanced on her lap and stared at me, bemused at my silly antics.

"Borrón y cuenta nueva." Scratch out and start again, Mami would say when I needed to abandon a school effort and start over again. Leaving Atiquizaya was like that: Borrón. Leave behind Abuela, Tío Samuel, Tía Valeria, Cornelia, Lauro, Glenda, Yuri, all my cousins, the entire teeming family hive living in Barrio el Ángel. Cuenta nueva: new school, new uniforms, new house, new street, new town.

Santa Ana was Mami's stomping grounds. She and her nine siblings reached adulthood under the shadow of the cerro to the north of town called Sihuatehuacán—Náhuat for "place of women" or "place of sorcerers." Our maternal abuela, or Abue, shared a home with Tía Salma and her four children, Josué, Joel, Sandra, and Ana. I was looking forward to seeing more of my cousin Josué. He was only nineteen days older than me, and we got along like siblings. I looked up to his sister Sandra, who was two years older than us. She was a force of nature. She practiced the piano diligently every afternoon, was an honor student, and kept her bedroom and affairs in meticulous order. To visit them from our new house, we'd need to walk for forty minutes through the heart of the city, which meant a stroll by the city's celebrated cathedral, where hundreds of doves thrived in its tall spears, pecking, shitting, and fluttering incessantly on its plaza. Camila and I ran straight into them to watch them flap, flitter, and flee into the cathedral's famous spires.

Cuenta nueva: One moment we were living in a venerable old house of tall adobe walls, red clay tiles, and a courtyard filled with birdsong, and in the next we were in a small three-bedroom brick house, with a backyard a fraction of the outdoor space we'd enjoyed in the old house. For the first time, our family would sleep in separate spaces. When I asked, since there were three bedrooms, if Camila and I could sleep separately, Papá said no. We were sisters and needed to learn to share because we only had each other, he explained. He always said the same thing: Learn to share, you only have each other. Over the years it all sounded like blah, blah, blah.

The move was swift. Camila and I were not even granted a chance to pack our things. Mami left us in Abue's care in Santa Ana for a few days, and when we walked into the new house for the first time, our things were already installed, except that my purple stuffed bear was not sitting on my bed and neither was the blue, green, and red striped rebozo my abuela had given me. No one bothered to ask us children what we needed, what we liked, what we wanted to keep, or if we wanted to move at all. I knew I would eventually see Cornelia, Abuela, and Tía Valeria again, but I was sure I would not see my bear or the cheerful woolen rebozo that had been a blanket, tablecloth, hammock, rug, veil, a faithful companion who knew the script to my childhood games.

Our new school, Madre de El Salvador, was run by Maryknoll nuns from the United States, and to my amazement and delight, it had a library. There were no public libraries in our little town, nor in Santa Ana. By the time we arrived at Madre de El Salvador, I already liked books very much and the stacks of books and wooden shelves at Madre de El Salvador became my first insight into what a library could look like. Our bookshelves at home were no comparison to entire walls, floor to ceiling, teeming with books. Most of the books at home were Papá's, but I had a few volumes of my own—not many, but enough to entertain me and make me dream of faraway places where menacing forests led to strange houses where bad things happened to children who managed by their own wits to rescue themselves.

In our new city, Mami subscribed me to a book-of-the-month club. This is how I discovered Jules Verne's excellent adventures of daring and extraordinary travels and Juan Ramón Jiménez's unforgettable *Platero y yo. Ben Hur, The Odyssey,* and *The Iliad* were also among the titles I came to own. I read their abridged versions and even then, the stories went completely over my head. Papá sometimes teased me by saying that I really needed to read the long versions of those stories, and just the thought it brought revulsion to my face and stomach.

As it was, I was not the only one enraptured with the school library. My classmates also eagerly anticipated the weekly library visit. Our favorite section was a corner of the downstairs stacks where *Las aventuras de Tintín* were shelved. On library day we raced down the steps to grab whatever Tintín books were not checked out. After raiding the shelf, the haggling began: I'll trade you this one for the one you have. The unlucky ones moved on to find a second-best option until our next library visit. This is how an adaptation of the legend of Genoveva de Brabante came to burrow in my heart. I read the story of the Lady treacherously banned from her court and forced to survive alone in the forest with her infant son. I admired Genoveva's grit and determination to survive, to do everything she could to safeguard her little boy, how she made a home in the forest and befriended deer, squirrels, foxes, and other animals, and how they protected her in turn. I loved the book so much I committed passages to memory.

In our new neighborhood, Camila and I made friends with Rebeca and Pati, who lived directly behind our house. Pati's parents were nice and low-key, but Rebeca's parents were downright fun. Her mom was a teacher like my parents and, like them, she was also studying at the Sede Occidental de la Universidad de El Salvador. When we arrived in Santa Ana both of my parents decided to further their education. Papá pursued a degree in biology and Mami a degree in English. The English degree was shorter than the licenciatura my father sought. In addition to her interest in the English language Mami wanted to teach at the high school level, and the language degree would permit her to reach her goal in a few years.

Rebeca's father was a professional fútbol player, like my own Tío Marcelo. From her family I learned that the original owner of our house had been a rather famous player on the national soccer team, which explained the two brick columns crowned with concrete soccer balls that flanked our front garden entrance.

Things were looking up in Santa Ana; I really liked my new school and our new friends, but despite the city's excitement and the house's indoor plumbing and modern layout, it could never replace Atiquizaya or the house we left behind. I missed the tall and thick adobe walls and refreshing tile floors whose cream swirls on a green background I had internalized from hours spent playing jacks with cousins and neighbors. In the old house, our lives were lived outdoors, in the corridor, in the garden spaces and large backyard where Papá tended his flowers, shrubs, and mature trees. I yearned for the roses, mallows, zinnias, figs, the mint shrubs scattered throughout. I missed our trees: the regal mango, the oranges, chirimoyas, jocotes, avocados, and bananas. The oregano sprawling on the side of the house, releasing its pungency in the early afternoon. The loroco vine that crawled its way up the reedy pomegranate. The leggy chipilines all the way in the back, whose fragrant small leaves were ever ready for harvesting. And the potted albahaca and yerba buena, stalwart soup companions, awaiting just outside the kitchen door. I missed the tacuazines, the lizards, and the prehistoric-looking garrobos sunning on our red tiles. I missed the myriad birds that flocked to our garden. I resigned myself to never meeting Cipitío, as we didn't have a wood stove in Santa Ana. Saddest yet, the new yard lacked the nooks and secret spaces necessary to escape from Papá's classical music, or to recover from shame on those occasions when Papá's anger overtook him, and he unleashed his belt to discipline us.

I missed my abuela. I missed knowing that she was in the house across the street from mine. I missed her roundness, her openness to my presence. I missed the aura of her home—redolent of sugar and freshly split coconuts—the darkness of the room where she slept, the religious figures on the walls hugged by shadows, the altar with the images of Saint Jude and the Sacred Heart of Jesus, the smell of rue, and the candlelight reflected in the glass of water on her nightstand. Back in Atiquizaya, at the end of my school day, I'd find Abuela in her house dispensing orders to get the manufacturing of sweets and candies underway after a long day selling her confections at her market stall. As a merchant, she had a constant stream of people coming and going from the house, bringing raw materials, working for a few hours, or simply stopping by for a greeting. Her house buzzed with life and her disposition and laughter cut through the days' ordeals and mundanity; it cut even through the disappointments.

In our final years in Atiquizaya Camila and I had become very close to Doña Elba and Don Galo's oldest daughters: Yuri and Glenda. Don Galo was a shoemaker and Doña Elba, a spice merchant. The two of them worked their respective trades in the front room of their house, and though they lived in harmony, there was a constant tug between the aromas in that front room: ground cinnamon curving around the edges of freshly polished shoes, nutmeg sheening over uncut leather, oregano and thyme knocking past jars of dye. Earthly smells darting around the volatile smells of glue and chemical dyes. In the evenings, the women worked carefully, weighing spices, scooping them into small plastic baggies, and sealing these over an open candle flame. They taught me how to sear the baggies, the gentle candlelight illuminating my face as I got closer to it, the plastic shrinking in a second, cowering from the heat. During the day, anyone passing by their house could see Don Galo hunched over his workstation, sinking tacks, affixing heels, buffing shoes.

Glenda was tall and slender with a fair complexion and reddish hair. She had a quietness about her, a shyness to her gaze. Yuri was shorter with square shoulders, dark hair, vivacious dark eyes, and a sharp tongue. She was spontaneous and full of mischief. Glenda and Yuri were older teenagers and like big sisters to Camila and me. In their company I learned some of the "secrets" women kept. One early afternoon I found Glenda on her bed covered with sheets, curled into herself. I could not understand why she would be in bed at the hottest time of the day. Yuri told me Glenda was on her period and experiencing cramps. Glenda's demeanor scared me a bit, but Yuri assured me Glenda would soon feel better, especially after drinking a tea her mother had brewed for her. Glenda presented as more delicate in body and temperament. Yuri took after her tireless and energetic mother, Elba.

Doña Elba had once invited me to come along on one of her spice distribution runs. We left the bus stop in Atiquizaya at dawn. At that hour morning dew still covered the world. She carried on her head a wide-mouth basket replete with the spices she had weighed and packaged the night before. She also carried spices in bulk and a diminutive balance that she used to weigh powders and seeds. Chalchuapa was our first stop. This was the same town where my abuela had her market stand. As the bus rolled into town, a birthing cow blocked the road. Cars and buses lined up one behind the other until the calf was strong enough to follow its mother and cross the two-lane highway. Minutes later we were walking over Chalchuapa's cobblestone streets. Then, on a quiet corner, Doña Elba went rigid and let out a long sigh. Astonished, I watched as a thick golden stream flowed from between her legs. She said nothing. When done, she picked up her stride and we walked over to a tienda, a small corner store, where she made her first sale of the day. There the smell of dried oregano and comino mingled with the toasted smell of dried grains: maíz and frijoles rojos stored in burlap sacks at the front of the room. That day we rode several regional buses and visited many tiendas, where she met longstanding clients and used her persuasive skills to make new ones. Sometimes she'd get requests for particular spices to bring next time, sometimes she'd use her balance to weigh out spices in bulk, sometimes she begged for people to take a single bag or small amounts of her spices. Her work was hard. It was dusk when we stepped out of the bus that brought us back to Atiquizaya.

Women were the pillars of my life in Atiquizaya: Doña Elba and her daughters. Doña Merced, the mother of my dear cousins. My tías and Abuela. My mami. The women who worked at our house looking after Camila and me. All of them made space for me in their lives. The men seemed to walk on a different lane to which I was scarcely invited. One of these women, Doña María, had taken care of Camila and me for years, and helped Mami with cleaning and cooking. Mami worked full-time as a grammar school teacher, and when Doña María left our employ Mami needed help to run the household. It was common practice then, as it is to this day, to hire a muchacha to look after young children, clean house, make meals, wash and iron. Mami hired different women to replace Doña María but some of them worked for a day, maybe two, then simply did not return. When there was no one to help, Glenda and Yuri stepped in.

The arrangement was to last only a few days until Mami could find permanent help, but one day ran into the next. We liked having Glenda and Yuri with us, and they liked working for us enough to stay on. Glenda arrived in the morning, then attended a sewing academy in the afternoon. Yuri, who attended school in the morning, changed posts with her sister in the afternoon. Bathing under the mango tree with the cold water Papá gathered from the public fountain the night before was not so bad with one of them lading the liquid over our heads, switching from nothing stories to ancient stories, chisme and lore.

We all missed Atiquizaya, yet in even in Santa Ana some things remained as they had been. Papá still followed the news cycle with the two newspapers he bought each day: *La Prensa* in the morning and *El Mundo* in the afternoon. My papá, in addition to being a teacher and a gardener, was also a news junkie. Our almuerzo often went like this: one bite of food, one gulp of the baritone voice reading the midday news on the radio, one bite of rice, the droning voice of the same man reading the next story. Kidnappings, ransoms, and takeovers of embassies in San Salvador in exchange for political prisoners became our new midday litany. Reports of ambushes and assassinations of important and not-so-important people gradually increased. Judges, business owners, teachers, students, someone standing at a bus stop, all were targets of the rising political violence.

A new routine was born in Santa Ana: Most Saturdays Papá traveled, often by train, back to Atiquizaya to visit Abuela and Tía Valeria. Sometimes he took us along. We walked from our home, past the cathedral in town center to the train station, doing our best to keep up with his long strides. We brought little with us because after lunch, when we took our leave, without fail, we were loaded with mangoes, jocotes, guayabas, candies, coffee, toys, remedies, syrups, all the things Abuela stashed away for us during the week. Looking back, I realize Abuela's gift giving was her way to soften the disappointment of not having us around.

The train was a lumbering relic, rocking from side to side like a hammock under a tree. The wooden floors in the passenger cars were deeply worn; in some places the floor planks had long cracks in them and we could see through down to the rails passing by. I relished the heavy noise of the engine chugging along its tracks, the grinding of steel upon steel. When we rolled through green tunnels, mature branches flapped against the sides of the wagons and tender sprouts managed their way in through open windows. *Hello!* they said, almost slapping our hands with glee.

I enjoyed the journey, except for the time it took the train to pull away from the outskirts of Santa Ana. Along this stretch, makeshift houses with desperation emanating from every door and window lined the path of the rail lines. The hovels were erected and shored up with scraps of sheet metal, corrugated tin, cardboard, sticks, canvas pieces, any sturdy material that afforded inhabitants a modicum of privacy and could keep out the rain and blistering sun. These homes were terrifying in their brittleness and precarity. Along the train tracks, older children stood next to their younger siblings. They watched transfixed as the train chugged along to destinations far, far away from them.

On one of those trips, Camila and I returned with parcels wrapped in newsprint that protected two gypsum images of the Virgin Mary from chipping. The icons were washed in a brassy gold tint to give them an aged look. When she gave them to us, Tía Valeria told us they had come from the market in Chalchuapa. Abuela bought them to protect and watch over us in our sleep, Tía Valeria told us. Camila and I were so pleased we hammered nails above our bed headboards as soon as we arrived home.

They hung on the wall in our room for weeks before Papá noticed them. One day as he came out of the shower, he stood in our bedroom's door, water trickling onto his forehead from his wet hair. "¿Qué esta haciendo esa mierda allí?" he demanded. I looked up at the "shit" he was pointing to. I turned to face him, and a flash of cold sweat spread through my back. I didn't like to see my papá upset. I had been on the receiving end of his searing belt enough times to know that tears didn't make welts go away. My eyes darted toward Camila, playing with her dolls on the floor between our beds, but she pretended not to hear anything. I mustered courage and responded that Tía Valeria had given them to us to protect our dreams.

Safe dreams or not, Papá's rigid stance under the door's frame told me he had a different opinion. A grunt escaped him. I looked over at Camila. This time she nodded in agreement as she fidgeted with the doll on her lap. At that moment I wished that whatever was running through his mind was not a belting, please. The way I saw it, I was always the one chosen for a spanking.

"Do you want us to take them down?" I asked shyly. Papá looked straight at me, his dark eyes boring into mine. "¡Solo son babosadas ustedes!" he grumbled, turned around, and disappeared down the hall. "Nonsense" he called it, our gesture to hang the icons according to our tía's instructions. Abuela and Tía Valeria believed ghosts lurk at night snatching people's souls. Camila and I didn't want our souls snatched. When she finally spoke, Camila murmured, "¡Nos salvamos!" The suggestion of a smile registered on her face and though I could not see it, I felt one registering on mine. We were saved.

8

The Body Remembers Even When the Mind Forgets

Oakland, California, 2003

After the shooting, my hands started to peel and fray. Deep cuts appeared, especially on my thumb and middle fingers, and they irked, and bled and stung. This condition had first started during the last years we spent in El Salvador. Over time I'd come to realize that whenever my stress levels or anxiety rose, my hands reflected the degree of my inner wretchedness.

In El Salvador I'd learned to carry out tasks carefully to prevent any irritations to my skin. Not knowing anything about allergies, I attributed the cuts and occasional bleeding to the incessant dust that kicked up on the streets. Mine was an allergy to dust, I told myself. But as the violence in the country intensified, my hands responded by splitting and tearing more. They became a barometer, a visceral map that mirrored the worsening situation on the streets. The violence we endured had no official name yet, but in the glossary of our every day it was quickly approaching the end of the alphabet, where *w*'s live and where war resides.

My hands were a harbinger of our lives' arrival at this archive entry of our Salvadoran history. Each of our bodies reacted in some way to the increasing tension and fear. Even months after our arrival in the United States, Mami often fell sick to her stomach and Papá suffered insomnia and persecution nightmares. Camila was the youngest and most sheltered. I had my hands. The day we landed at Miami airport, our port of entry into the US, the cuts in my fingers were deep enough that the officer that processed our papers at the INS office inside the airport grew increasingly frustrated by the poor quality of my fingerprints. He did not hide his distaste as he rejected form after form because after he inked and rolled the tips of my fingers, he faced jagged, choppy prints not the smooth whorls he expected to see.

Back in Oakland, John, like my hands, insisted that something was not well, and I eventually found the courage to call our insurance company. Yes, they do offer mental health services, a cheerful voice on the line said, and by the way, the voice added, I qualified for individual and group therapy. A beige two-story building on Berkeley's busy Telegraph Avenue, a stone's throw from Aurora's pediatrician, turned out to house the mental health clinic to which I was referred. I arrived on time for the appointment, checked in with the receptionist and took a seat. My name was called. I walked down the length of a dark corridor past closed doors, imagining patients behind them struggling to tell their truths just like I was about to do. Behind my assigned door, a white-bearded man sat on a swivel chair; a banker's lamp on a dark desk spilled a pool of warm light. He motioned for me to sit on a deep-maroon sofa. I did so with unease, feeling the couch give in to my weight, which was a fraction of the heaviness that pressed on my shoulders.

The therapist asked what had brought me there. I decided to risk everything and start at the beginning. I told him I was from El Salvador, that I had lived there during the build-up to the Salvadoran Civil War. That I saw armed fights on the street, buses consumed by flames, that I saw bombs exploding and corpses on the streets, that for years I had lived with the fear that my father would be targeted and killed. I explained how the violence in front of my house had torn open something in me, broken a dam, and let a gush of memories rush out.

Our lives in El Salvador were marked by fear so strong, I said, that just the idea of returning to the country for a visit filled me with terror. I had returned to El Salvador only once in twenty years, I said, even though I longed to be part of it, to smell its smells, taste its foods, see my cousins and aunts, visit the house I grew up in, and meet family members born in our absence. At times tears threatened to disrupt my telling. As I spoke, his face remained neutral, and his hand took notes on a yellow pad. Now and then he scratched his beard. When I was done, he looked squarely at me.

"Well, you have suffered a trauma, but with a few visits you will see that you will feel better," he said. Whatever he said next couldn't make it through the maelstrom inside my head. I stared back at him from the bottom of the sofa where I had sunk.

Did he not hear what I had just said?

Did he not see what it cost me to say it?

Did he just tell me I would feel better with a few visits?

Who was he kidding?

Not me.

My goal in reaching out to a therapist was to tease out the disruptive feelings and thoughts related to El Salvador that I was experiencing in the shooting's aftermath. The therapist had only heard the Oakland story. Suddenly, the office felt small and claustrophobic. I looked down at the floor, saw my toenails staring back at me from my red sandals. *This guy doesn't get it,* I told myself; *he does not get it at all.* When the session was over, I shut the door behind me and walked back down the long corridor, back into daylight, shaken by my daring. For the first time I had admitted to another person, but most importantly to myself, that I had lived through a war.

Guerra is not only the grotesque moments, the violence of killing others. Guerra affects those living in the context of the violence. There is no periphery to Guerra. Guerra doesn't go away when the bullets stop or when helicopter blades no longer spin. Guerra stays inside of you like a dormant illness. Guerra comes and assaults you over and over, again and again, and your body erupts each time, inflaming your insides, sometimes cutting up your hands.

The words I had spoken in the man's office stuck to the roof of my mouth. At some point during our meeting, I'd flown out of my body and another me spoke things I'd never shared before. I did not understand all of the complications of what was happening to me. But I knew enough to know a few visits would not take away the loss, sorrow, and whatever else ran rampart inside me. With my head spinning and a knot in my stomach, I walked away knowing I would never sit in that sofa again.

9

A Teacher's Life

May the families of the assassinated teachers know that I feel close to them, that I share their pain, that I keep in my prayers their loved ones so violently torn from them and all of you who inconsolably cry for them. My thoughts also go to all of you, teachers, for whom threats and intimidation make it impossible to live and work in peace.

—Óscar Romero, Archbishop of San Salvador

Santa Ana, El Salvador, 1978–1979

The news of kidnappings and ransoms that we had been hearing on the radio gave way to darker, sordid headlines of embassy bombings, church occupations, priest killings, burning factories. Terror coiled itself around our lives one event at a time, each more sinister than the last. The news traveled from one home to the other, people spoke sotto voce, as if using a normal tone of voice could make the horror real. As if it ever could be more real than it already was.

The red phone in our living room rang. Josué called. He called me sometimes, sometimes I called him. We'd spend hours on the phone, to our mothers' annoyance. We had lots to talk about, as we were the same age and in the same grade. We tutored each other on math problems and other school assignments; we discussed TV shows and masterminded the games we'd play the next time our families would see each other. But this time when the red phone rang it was not Josué on the other side of the line. The call came from Atiquizaya to inform us that Papá's good friend, Señor Cabrera, principal of the school in Atiquizaya where Papá had taught and I had attended, had been murdered. Murdered in his favorite rocking chair as he read the afternoon newspaper. His mother was in the adjacent room, making dinner. The front door of his house was open to let light in, as was his custom. It took the killers seconds

Engine left idling, jump out of pickup,
step via open door into living room, aim, shoot
—to obliterate a brilliant mind.

He knew he was marked, Papá said. He had quit his work at the school and for a while moved to live with relatives in San Salvador, hoping to divert his stalkers. But when he returned, the death squads were waiting for him. It was known that Señor Cabrera belonged to ANDES, and it was public knowledge that it was the death squads who killed him. Teachers, my papá often said, were targeted because they were thought to plant seeds of insurrection in their students. "They think we are turning kids into guerrilleros," my father would say, and shake his head. "They blame us, but anyone who has eyes and thinks for themselves can see what is in front of them. No one is inventing the miseries of our lives," he'd say.

I overheard my parents' conversations, the stories of teachers' murders. These anecdotes transformed into agitated hornets buzzing, restless, in my head. My parents spoke in hushed tones among themselves and with other adults to protect us, but the toxicity of the violence they described lingered in the room and hung suspended like pollutant particulate, eventually finding its way into my lungs. When Señor Cabrera was killed, my parents and everyone who attended his funeral did so at the risk of their own lives because the death squads had orejas por todos lados—informants—all over the place.

In a conversation decades later, Tía Maura shared with me how a friend of hers had lived through a neighbor's assassination. My aunt's friend lived on the same street as a couple who were both teachers. My aunt told me how armed men raided the couple's house in the middle of the night and dragged and killed the man outside while his wife and children were inside. Another day, Papá told me that in the town of Turín, between Atiquizaya and Ahuachapán, a well-known teacher was torn from his classroom and killed outside the school by a group of armed men.

Tía Valeria shared with me another similar story. A forceful knock in the late evening at Señor M.'s house alerted the family that something was wrong. Señor M. taught at the same school where Señor Cabrera had been principal and where my papá had taught. A group of men pulled him onto the street and tied his hands with a rope, which in turn was tied to a car. The men drove away, dragging Señor M. through Atiquizaya's uneven cobblestone streets. When he was eventually untied, he was executed. His body was abandoned on the spot.

These stories accumulated. Sometimes teachers' deaths showed up in newspapers. Sometimes we heard them via word of mouth. Teachers targeted by death squads. Most of my parents' friends and many of their acquaintances were teachers. Some of them were murdered.

One killing story at a time, I began to understand that if my parents' friends had been assassinated then surely my parents could be too. The time of Hush had arrived. *Shh*, people's eyes said. *Shh*, their mouths said. The walls in our houses, the wooden shutters of our windows *Shh*, they whispered. *Shh*, said the water we drank. *Shh*, clouded daytime, nighttime, dream time, all the time.

On one of my visits back to El Salvador decades later, over coffee and salpores, Papá and Tía Valeria remembered teachers' marches they had participated in.

"¿Es que no te acordás, Roman?" Tía asked, and in his measured fashion Papá responded barely shaking his head, no.

"Si hombre, marchamos en Atiquizaya y vos te subiste al kiosco y te dirigiste al grupo. ¿No te acordás?" "Come on!" she insisted, not letting him avoid the conversation so easily.

Tía Valeria was referring to an episode when she and my papá and dozens of teachers, members of ANDES, marched through the streets of Atiquizaya. He'd led the march and later addressed the crowd from the kiosk of the town's central park.

"Ah sí hombre, esa onda, ese día, fue gremial la cuestión, no fue política." It was a labor union rally, Papá says, not a political one. They marched to demand changes to the teacher retirement system. Santa Ana and San Salvador also saw marches on the same day. Across the country there were marches, said Papá, who was now lost in full-blown reminiscing.

"Y las vendedoras salieron de los puestos a aplaudirnos cuando pasamos por el mercado, ¿te acordás?" my tía added. Sí, my dad agreed, the women from the market did support the marching teachers in Atiquizaya, unlike the ones in Ahuachapán, who pelted them with rotten eggs as they passed in front of their mercado.

In the safety of the moment from which we looked back, we all laughed at the image of the Ahuachapán market women—known for their incendiary tempers—in their wide aprons and plastic sandals, lashing out, bombarding clean-cut teachers with stinky eggs. "We wondered," Papá said, "where in heavens they had managed to find so many rotten eggs!"

Papá then shared how hard it had been to travel to Ahuachapán on that particular day because the local authorities were tipped off to the Atiquizaya teachers' plan to travel en masse to support their colleagues. The police set up a roadblock and diverted cars driven by teachers and stopped and searched buses, forcing teachers to get off. There is only one two-lane road that connects the two towns, and it is well transited. Just beyond Ahuachapán is a border crossing with Guatemala. Papá and his colleagues did not give up. They simply started walking the twelve kilometers to get there.

They made it to the march just in time, he said, because the driver of a big rig on his way to Guatemala asked them if they'd like a lift inside his transport container. They piled in and rode in the dark, in the stale air, like contraband. "Pero aquí esa vez fue feo," interjected Tía Valeria, noting how it got ugly when they returned to Atiquizaya because they came to find a big, red-haired dog strangled and left hanging from the threshold of the Teacher's House in Atiquizaya. Ugliness and violence had accompanied teachers for years before the death squads started targeting them. Since the late 1960s they have been the largest worker's rights organization El Salvador has ever known. They successfully, peacefully, marched to demand better salaries, job security, medical services, good working conditions, and retirement. For this, they were despised and killed.

Back in Santa Ana Mami asked Papá to stop his weekend visits to Atiquizaya to check on his family, my abuela, and Tía Valeria. It had become too dangerous to travel. It was by then routine for government forces to stop buses traveling between cities and search passengers for any evidence linking them to any government opposition group. Uniformed officials asked passengers to exit and stand in a straight line facing the side of the bus, their backs to the men who searched their bodies and possessions. A book with a political title or a flyer to a march or rally were enough to justify an arrest, which later could become a disappearance.

The fear we felt splintered us from Atiquizaya and gave way to yet another routine: Instead of visiting Abuela in Atiquizaya, we now visited Abue, my mami's mom, who lived with Tía Salma. Every Sunday afternoon we walked as a family from the corner of Santa Ana where we lived across town to Colonia IVU. While the adults settled down for coffee and pan dulce under the grape arbor, us children busied ourselves with made-up games. Papá had planted the grape arbor years before. When he put it in the ground, it was a lonely stick, but over time, and with his care, it grew into a fruiting vine. He built a crisscross pattern across half the center courtyard using wire and trained the grape's tendrils to a form a leafy shelter. With time the vines yielded sweet purple grapes. They hung in generous bunches every December, adding panache to the end-of-year festivities. The rest of the year the pleasant arbor offered shade to all who sat beneath it. Papá did that: planted trees, vines, and flowering bushes at other people's houses. It was his signature. He birthed a string of sweet children in the form of ripe guavas, mangoes, avocados, squashes, and always roses.

My cousin Sandra had become too old and sophisticated to bother with the games her younger brother Josué, Camila, and I played. The three of us saw eye to eye in most things and understood the importance of experimentation: We concocted recipes and blended ingredients for the world's most undrinkable smoothies, ignited vile perfume and cologne cocktails, constructed elaborate insect hospitals with spent matchboxes, created games with such intricate rules we lost our way inside them. When Camila and I spent the weekend at

Abue and Tía Salma's house, we took epic showers, the three of us, singing, posing, stomping, marching, and giving speeches for hours on end under the wide shower head.

Once, as a way of getting back at Sandra for not playing with us anymore, the three of us abducted a few dolls from her miniature doll collection. She had amassed a fair number of two-inch dolls with outsized heads and colorful hair down to their ankles. We borrowed a kitchen knife, scrounged around for small paper boxes we fashioned to resemble coffins, stuffed the dolls inside them, and snuck across the street, where there was a field overrun with grasses and scrawny self-seeded tomato plants.

Out in the field we dug a hole large enough to deposit the little boxes with the dolls inside, dusted dirt on top, and took turns stabbing them. Sometimes the tip of the knife jammed up against a side of a carboard box. Undeterred and sweating, we dislodged it and went on with our diabolical game. We hunched over with laughter when Sandra, unaware of our game and intention, stood on the front balcony and waved to us a friendly hello. We waved back with maniacal mirth, dirt smudged on our hands and faces, and caked under our fingernails. For the most part the dolls were in perfect shape when we finally pulled them out of the boxes. The cardboard had absorbed the knife's impact. Just one or two had a bit of hair lopped off, another had a slight cut on the side of her face. These injuries were hardly noticeable and besides, Sandra, already well in puberty's grip, hardly played with her dolls anymore, or with us for that matter.

We children witnessed violence against bodies and against property. The collective fear, among our relatives and acquaintances, the fear to speak thoughts and feelings freely, became a kind of violence in and of itself. No one dared speak in the open about what they experienced or saw. In the countryside, campesinos were murdered, in cities and in rural areas, teachers were murdered, young people too, and marches were disrupted with clubs and bullets. The word "situación" started making an appearance in our daily lexicon. Labeling the violence and strife as a "situation" turned it into a distant thing, something unattributable, a silent menace. I believe that the very vagueness of the term permitted us to go on with our lives. But it was clear that the situación corroded nervous systems, gave headaches, stomachaches, and made people pray.

I knew Mami feared for Papá as he continued to be involved with the national teacher's union. She worried also because the few courses they had left to graduate were only offered at the national university campus in San Salvador. Mami took afternoon classes and returned early in the evening. Papá taught the afternoon shift and took evening classes. He returned from San Salvador at night, on increasingly late buses. Sometimes he did not return at all and would choose to spend the night with friends and acquaintances.

"Ay, Dios mío," Mami said every time Papá shared a new story. "Ay no. Demasiado peligroso."

"That road from San Salvador to Santa Ana is already so dangerous with all the curves, crags, and cliffs, and now with the bus searches and kidnappings," she'd say. Once, on a trip to San Salvador with her, just the two of us, I witnessed the dangers of that particular stretch of road. The bus was relatively empty; there was no one standing in the aisles or carrying someone on their lap, as was common when the buses were filled beyond capacity. We sat in a three-person seat, Mami in the middle, keeping me away from the stranger at the window. I encircled my mother's arm and rested my head on it. The tender softness of the inner arm and the pillowy thickness of the upper arm lulled me as we rolled along the twisty carretera. The bus motored loudly up hills, lurched and listed as it hugged the tight curves. Our bodies leaned tightly right or left with the inertia. With each curve, I nuzzled Mami's arm for comfort, but I also felt her anxiety. At one point, she leaned over me into the aisle and, raising her voice over the engine's drone, implored the conductor to slow down, "¡Señor, maneje más despacio por favor, es demasiado peligroso!"

More and more often, when she spoke to Papá, she brought up the violence, not her fear of the road itself. "It is not worth it to keep going to San Salvador for classes," she said, "I'd rather us move than expose ourselves like this."

Yet among the increasing fear, we had a moment of brightness in our lives. In a welcome turn of events, Atiquizaya returned to us. Lauro, who was by now a teacher, started coming by for short visits, and Doña Corina—who was the mother of Señor Diógenes, one of Papá's childhood friends—came to help with the house and take care of Camila and me. Lauro was older and more serious but always kind, and he and Papá would sit in the living room and talk for what seemed like hours. Doña Corina was like Abuela in many ways: rotund and jolly, with the habit of wearing aprons with large deep pockets on top of her dresses and skirts.

"¿Ya llegaron?" she'd say when we returned from school. "Tell me what happened today." Before one of us uttered a sound, she'd flick a paring knife and start—*chas, chas*—deftly peeling—*chas, chas*—whatever fruit she had brought from Atiquizaya that morning, but not without first savoring the weight of the fruit in her hand, admiring its coloration, and taking in its perfume. A green mango, a young cucumber, an arrayán. Camila and I jostled to be the first to sink our teeth into the peeled fruit. We liked coming home to her and her spicy stews. But one day Doña Corina simply stopped coming. Traveling from Atiquizaya to Santa Ana by bus every morning proved to be too much for her at her age.

Things changed with Lauro as well. As time went by his visits became irregular and sometimes furtive. He had gotten more and more involved with the movement, I overheard Papá say. He had gone underground and taken a pseudonym. When Lauro visited, the two of them talked about things Mami was increasingly unhappy about. I overheard her telling Papá that Lauro should not visit us anymore. People might be following him. "Things are getting dangerous, Roman!" she said. "They're saying at work that teachers are being cased out, for later. They are taking people away, Roman!"

I loved Lauro. He was gentle and understanding and always quick and ready to jump in on one of our street games. It didn't matter if it was béisbol, hide-and-seek, a tag marathon, or singing rounds, he joined us with energy and good humor. On one occasion, Lauro walked into my house in Atiquizaya at the precise moment Doña Maria was admonishing me. I was in the corridor of our house facing the rose garden, crying while she wagged her finger at me. Lauro simply asked, "¿Qué pasa aquí?" Caught off guard, Doña María spun on one foot and walked away. Lauro knew Doña María because she also lived in Atiquizaya. He knew she was well-meaning but stern. He scooped me up and sat me on the half wall dividing the corridor from the rose garden. It was late afternoon and Lauro must have been returning from his teaching job. He wore a short-sleeve button-down shirt neatly tucked into his trousers and carried a pen in the left pocket as Papá often did. Sitting on the half wall brought me almost eye to eye with him. It was easy to talk to him. In a few minutes of conversation the scolding from Doña María dissipated from my mind, leaving instead only my love and appreciation for Lauro.

"Lo tuve que hacer, Roman." I had to do it, Mami said to Papá after dinner, after taking a long drag of her cigarette. "Tengo miedo." I am afraid, Mami said. Plain and simple. This is why she and two of her close colleagues at the school where she taught kindergarten visited the alcaldía after work to request that their cédulas, their IDs, list their professions as "homemaker" instead of "teacher." "Imagine being pulled from a bus with our cédulas listing 'teacher' as our profession?" she said, holding Papá's gaze. He nodded. "Sí, hicistes bien, Inez. ¿Qué más podemos hacer?" You did well. What else can be done? was my papá's answer.

I remember Papá after an evening conversation with Mami, walking over to the open front door. His short-sleeve button-down shirt was untucked, as was his habit when at home, his thin feet inserted in his rubber house sandals. I see his slender frame standing in the door's threshold. His fingers loosely interlaced behind his back, he looked straight out into the garden, into the shadows, past the soccer balls at our gate, and toward the greater darkness of faraway stars and their faint light, before he let out a long sigh.

The great eye up in the sky would have seen Papá standing there, the stars responding with their intermittent shimmer. The eye would have seen Mami sitting in the living room on the rust-colored sofa, Camila in our bedroom, and me quietly lingering at the dining room table, my finger tracing the dainty marigolds stamped on the transparent plastic table covering. The four of us in our dimly illuminated brick house. The great eye surely saw each of us holding our places, balancing on the filament of history we were living.

Teachers were systematically identified, followed, and killed. They were killed in front of their families, in front of their students, on the way to the schools where they taught. This happened. It happened while we were in El Salvador. It happened to my parents' friends and the impact of this fact, despite the distance of years, does not lessen. We were floating on the swell of the wave that would soon crash our lives. "Tengo miedo"—I'm afraid—was a phrase Mami repeated frequently as news of the disappearances and murders of teachers increased.

It was at this time, on one of Tía Maura's visits from the United States for Christmas, that Mami had the first conversations with her about leaving the country. Tía Maura, Mami's youngest sister, had been living in the US since the early seventies and visited El Salvador every December. The days of her arrival and departure were feast days for our family. We drove cars and sometimes rented a van to take us to the national airport. Nothing was more sensational to me than to watch Tía Maura emerge from the airplane's door and descend the stairs onto the tarmac. She, like my mother, has always been a fashionable woman. In the 1970s she gave off serious Bianca Jagger vibes with her long, shiny dark hair and oversized sunglasses, a designer bag on her arm and platform shoes on her feet. Tía Maura was superlative in every way: bighearted, with a serious temper, exquisitely fashionable, and simply beautiful.

When she was in El Salvador, she turned Abue's house into her homebase, and the entire Luna clan camped there for the days leading up to Christmas. Abue enlisted everyone to help her prepare the great Christmas tamale feast. Under her strict guidance we toasted and ground spices, cubed, seasoned, and braised pork meat, stewed chicken, mixed pure cacao into her recaudo, cooked vats of masa on the stove top. Washing and preparing the banana leaves to wrap the tamales and then assembling them required focus and stamina but all of us agreed that Abue's tamales were the best ever made. Our Christmas started at sundown on the 24th of December and went on until sunrise of the 25th. The hours were spent dancing, eating tamales, and visiting friends. At midnight we exchanged gifts, then el reventón de pólvora (fireworks) followed. During those end-of-year festivities Tía Maura and Mami got talking and began planning how our family might escape the violence by emigrating to the US.

When the din of the holidays settled, I learned that Mami and Tía Maura had decided to move forward with their plan. Teachers continued to be killed. Anxiety overwhelmed me waiting for my parents to return from their classes. They balanced their teaching jobs with their university studies as best they could and this meant they were away from home most of the day. Camila and I were spending more time with our muchacha than with either of our parents. I felt a forever pit in my stomach. My mind refused to name it. I didn't want the red telephone in the living room to ring with bad news, like the news of Señor Cabrera.

Given the danger, my parents decided to move again, this time to San Salvador. The situation had grown too dangerous to travel back and forth between the two cities. By the time we left for San Salvador in early 1979, Tía Maura, from her home in Florida, had submitted the initial papers asking permission for Mami to immigrate. Because Mami was married, and both her children were under eighteen, Papá, Camila, and I also qualified under the same application. In the meantime, I would start eighth grade in a new school. New uniform. New house. New friends. New attitude. The very possible death or disappearance of my parents terrified me. But I was afraid to share my fear with anyone lest it come true, and I also didn't think that given the very serious situation we lived in, anyone would want to hear my concerns. All around me I saw that silencing oneself was a way to survive. *Shh*, I whispered to myself. *Shh*, seeped into my bones. *Shh*, borrón y cuenta nueva.

10

Truce

Oakland, California, 2004

After the failed visit to the therapist in Berkeley, I did my best to center the needs of my very pregnant body and the impending birth. I gave Aurora as much time as I could, knowing that her life, our life as a family, would soon be transformed. My body, and Aurora's needs demanded that I take one day at a time.

"Hay un bebé ahí!" I'd tell Aurora every time she showed interest in my growing belly. "Bebé!" she'd repeat, gently poking my round, taut stomach.

To Aurora, "baby," "bebé," was an abstraction. She repeated the word, but whether she understood another person was growing inside me was unclear. My soon-to-be-born baby loved to kick hard on the right side of my body—especially at night. By the seventh month of pregnancy, I carried out my days on teaspoons of sleep, unable to rely on caffeine to perk up as I normally would. The lack of sleep and severe acid reflux—a pregnancy side effect I'd also experienced with Aurora—kept me secure in my self-imposed coffee abstinence. I went to yoga classes, swam laps at the Oakland YMCA, hiked in the Oakland Hills to keep my body and mind alert and fit for the birth.

The new baby arrived three days before the due date. I'd swum laps at the Oakland YMCA in the midafternoon while Aurora was at preschool before I felt the first contractions soon after dinner that evening. John poured me a small glass of red wine and served me a second helping of pasta.

"You'll need the energy and the relaxation," he said.

Our second child was born shortly before noon the following day. He was a perfectly calm and healthy eight-pound baby. Mami, who was on standby in Southern California, took the first available flight to join us. We all looked forward to having Mami's bright spirit in the house. Aurora loved spending time with Abuelita, who doted on her shamelessly. In the few hours we had to ourselves before Mami arrived, John squeezed into my hospital bed, and I nestled the baby on his chest. We were whole and happy.

After a week Mami returned home. It is then that I slowly emerged from the fog of twenty-four-hour on-call nursing. Soon I was managing short walks and errands, pushing baby Izal in a stroller or carrying him in a canvas sling. Walking along Grand Avenue back to the car after a supermarket run, I stopped to read the real estate postings on the Prudential office window and on a whim ambled inside. It is a game, I told myself. I can pretend that I am interested in trading my house for a better one. John need not ever find out. Sell the old to buy new—people do it all the time.

"Please take a seat," the elegant woman inside said. She stood and gestured to the chair in front of her desk. I obliged. Izal was snug inside the sling. I spewed pleasantries to excuse my presence in her office and to give myself time to come up with a strategy, one that didn't wander far from the truth. "I own a house in North Oakland," I rambled on. "Our family is growing,"—I pointed to the baby in the sling—"and we are looking for a bigger place . . ."

What type of house am I looking for?

What is my price range?

What neighborhoods did I have in mind?

Have I had my current house appraised?

Do we have a loan secured?

I had no ready answers. My heart pounded inside my head, wanting to shout:

All I want is to move NOW!

"Why don't you give these questions some thought and, in the meantime, take a careful look at the listings I am about to print out for you," the agent said politely.

"Yes, that is a great idea," I said, thanking her for giving me an out.

"You can call or email me if anything draws your attention," she said, smiling, handing me her card. Tactful with her dismissal, she allowed me to save face without closing the door on the possibility that I may indeed be the owner of a house in North Oakland interested in purchasing a different home to fit my family.

What am you looking for? the real estate agent had asked.

What am I looking for? I asked myself.

At the playground near the bird estuary in Lake Merritt—not far from the realtor's office—watching flocks of geese and ducks flapping after breadcrumbs thrown by well-meaning visitors, I repeated under my breath: "What is it that I want? What am I looking for?" What rose to the forefront of my mind was what I didn't want: to feel my body tense up as I approached the corner of Dover and Aileen. I did not want to live through another neighborhood shooting. I didn't want the ghost of my scared self to haunt my nights.

What I wanted was a place where I could go on a neighborhood walk with my babies and my dog, not ambushes. I wanted a house with a big yard for growing flowers and vegetables. I needed a place with fertile soil to sink my hands into, a place where I could plant a tree and experience the joy of putting seeds in the ground season after season. I inherited, at best, a quarter of my father's green thumb, but a full measure of his love of plants and, above all, trees. From my park bench, watching sun and wind dance and ripple through tree branches, I eventually arrived where I knew I would: at an old adobe house with a red tiled roof.

I was looking for a house set on a deep, rectangular lot planted with abundant fruit trees, where the earth released its musty secrets after a good rain and where iguanas sunbathed on hot red tejas. In this house birds, bats, opossums, and other critters came and went, flying, scampering about their business. I wanted the call of beans cooking on the stove and the lure of cinnamon swirling in a pot of arroz con leche and a dog sleeping under a scrap of shade, its belly rising and falling to the echo of chickens pecking about. This house teemed with roses and was enchanted with the midday scent of orange and fig leaves. I wanted the Atiquizaya house I grew up in, but I wanted it here—in the US.

The house I searched for, my childhood home, still exists. My Aunt Valeria lives in it. Save for a few upgrades—a porcelain toilet and an enclosed shower—and minus a few of the large trees, it remains largely as it was when my family lived in it. Things have changed of course; the roses, oranges, and fig tree that Papá planted are gone from the central courtyard, and a spider as big as a hummingbird has woven an epic web over the space. "The tropics are generous," Papá always said—the warmth and rain could make things otherwise small swell to elephantine proportions. The magic of my childhood lives suspended between the thick adobe walls of that old house: watching chicks peck their eggshells, eager to begin their chicken lives, hearing the plop of ripe mangoes landing on soft ground, watching hefty rain drops create liquid crowns upon impact, playing jacks on cool, clean tiled floors, imbibing the pungent aroma of oregano on sweltering afternoons, watching colorful lizards doing push-ups under a fierce sun, going to bed with my mother, father, sister, in the same room, knowing that we would be together when the roosters called the new day . . . *Yes*, the house's adobe walls say, *all of that is still here, held by us.*

In the evening, over dinner, I told John.

"You'll never guess what I did today while out with Izal," I said, trying to find a way to ease into the conversation. "I poked my head into the Prudential office on Grand Ave. You know, the one next to Trader Joe's."

"You did, huh," he said, looking at me askance and putting down his fork. That night's dinner was a favorite of ours, pasta with homemade Bolognese simmered gently on the stove for hours.

"I mean, I went in just to check it out. A nice realtor sat down with me. She gave me some listings," I said, pointing at the stapled packet on the metal shelf next to the small kitchen table. "Told me to reach out if we saw anything we liked. I have her email."

"You're serious about this, huh?"

Our eyes met through our glasses. I nodded. "Well, I also have a surprise for you," he said, taking something out of the front pocket of his jeans. "I called a few folks. Remember Charles? He passed along the name of an Argentinian therapist up in Glenview. He spoke highly of her. She sounds like she could help you."

The last thing I wanted was to deal with a therapist. In my life I had dealt with two: the man I had recently visited in Berkeley and someone else I had seen many years earlier in Southern California, when I'd taken on a temporary job filling in for a social worker on maternity leave. I was familiar with social work, as I had done it straight out of college for a year. One afternoon, reading a report about a child with developmental disabilities, I became dizzy; letters broke out of order as if running away from the words they were supposed to represent. I read and reread the same sentence, unable to extract its meaning. I was worried enough by the experience that I made a mental health appointment with my provider.

The therapist I saw suggested I practice relaxation techniques and prescribed group therapy once a week. On my way out of the clinic, though the glass walls of the group therapy room, I saw some people sitting in a circle. In my youthful arrogance and ignorance, I decided such circles were not for me. I never went back to see the therapist. I figured that if I had a similar episode in the future, I would step outside, take in some fresh air, maybe have a cigarette to distract myself, and let the feeling pass.

John was staring at me expectantly waiting for my answer to his suggestion and I realized I'd become completely absorbed in my memory.

"Okay. I'll call," I said.

If I wanted him to consider looking at houses, I had to honor his request.

11

La Situación

San Salvador, El Salvador, 1980

If our move to Santa Ana felt, to Camila and I, like it was done in haste, the move to San Salvador felt like it was done in secrecy. Cornelia's prophecy pronounced years earlier at the top of our cobblestone street was unfolding as she had stated, in part driven by my parents' educational pursuits and in part by the rising violence. Newspaper headlines and radio bulletins reporting encounters, kidnappings, ransoms, murders, ambushes, explosions, were no longer in some undefined "over there," but "here." Day was day and night, night, but they were dimmer versions of what we had previously known. Above us a new lord orchestrated our days. Below us a new lord waited to swallow us up.

In San Salvador the sound of machine guns became as familiar as Atiquizaya's roosters summoning the dawn. In the tautness

---

January 1980

Jan. 4 – Approximately 30 individuals attacked the National Guard garrison. Two guardsmen and two civilians were killed.

Jan. 9 – The armed forces allow three civilians to reintegrate and form part of the ruling government, called Junta Revolucionaria de Gobierno.

Jan. 11 – Four leftist organizations (LP-28, BPR, FAPU, and UDN) signed a pact in the University of El Salvador. This new umbrella group will be henceforth known as el Comité Coordinador de la Unidad Revolucionaria.

---

of the streets, road blockades manned by combat-ready personnel were everywhere; army trucks packed with soldiers in combat gear patrolled at all hours. Spray painted slogans, "Revolución o Muerte," "Libertad para presos políticos," and countless acronyms, "FAPU" "BPR" "FPL" "UDN," jostled for the attention of the furtive eye that dared read them.

Our new house was in Colonia San Carlos, a leafy neighborhood west of the national university. Tío Javier, my mother's youngest brother, who was completing his medical residency at Hospital Rosales, the country's main hospital, and his girlfriend, Mónica, an ER nurse at the hospital, moved in with us. Reina, a muchacha recommended by Mónica, also moved in with us to take care of Camila and me and help with the domestic upkeep. Seven humans, a dog, a cat, a goldfish and, for a short while, an armadillo, came to live in this house which we inhabited for only a year.

The downstairs had spacious shared living spaces, a rectangular narrow patio with a solitary tree and, in the back wall, a niche, lined with white-and-azure tiles where normally a religious icon would rest. The upstairs had three bedrooms, the largest with its own balcony, and a large open terrace that Reina used for drying laundry. With its ample living and dining rooms, the house would have made for nice family gatherings. But we saw our extended family less and less. Months had gone by since I last saw my abuela, Tía Valeria, and Cornelia and her family.

While we were there Monina, a smooth-haired dachshund, gave us a litter and Frederick, our orange tabby—so baptized because he froze

---

Jan. 12 – The group LP-28 has seized the Costa Rican and Panamanian embassies and are holding hostages, demanding liberty for jailed group members.
Jan. 21 – Sixteen bombs exploded in San Vicente, in the eastern part of the country. Five members of the same family were murdered.

Jan. 21 – Civilians have seized churches in San Salvador and in the interior of the country as safe spaces following violent encounters.

in rapt attention any time Chopin came on Papá's record player—was ever our sweet companion. The fish with no name belonged to Mónica. She taught Camila and me how to care for it and clean its tank. One sunny afternoon I decided to clean the tank on the terrace. I left the tank alone for a second to run downstairs to grab the net we used to scoop out the fish. When I returned I found its orange sliver thrashing, half sizzling on the blistering tile. From then on it swam with three fourths of a tail.

*

When we arrived in San Salvador the school year had already started, and enrollment was closed at many schools. After much searching Mami enrolled me in eighth grade and Camila in four in Escuela España, a kindergarten-to-ninth-grade all-girls school. I liked it, but I think I would have liked any school. The alternative—to spend the rest of the year at home—would have been unbearable. Going to school, doing homework, interacting with classmates gave Camila and I something to look forward to. Even the ridiculous all-white uniform—a dress with a line of white buttons down the front, a white belt, and white knee-high socks—was preferable to staying home. We'd already lost many school days to teachers' national work stoppages, and to armed "encounters" between guerrillas and government forces.

Escuela España abutted the national university at the opposite end from where we lived. The shortest way to our new school was through

Jan. 21 – A bomb exploded in the BPR (Bloque Popular Revolucionario) headquarters in San Salvador.

Jan. 22 – Several dead and wounded in San Salvador after a demonstration by the groups UDN, LP-28, FAPU, and BPR was broken up with gunfire. Demonstrators took refuge in El Rosario Church and in the Metropolitan Cathedral, both downtown.

---

the campus. Political slogans, graffiti, and tags hollered from walls; huge protest canvases hung from the terraces and windows of the various faculty buildings. The campus had been attacked on more than one occasion, its walls visibly pocked marked with bullets. This was because the government viewed the university as a hotbed of radicalism, a citadel of Marxist teachings.

People could also be pockmarked with bullet holes. There was more than one way of saying "pockmarked with bullet holes."

acribillado

balaceado

pistoleado

tiro

ametrallado balaciar

bala tiroteado

matado a balas asesinado

baliado

matar muerto

Jan. 22 – On the same day of the shooting that led people to take refuge in churches downtown, armed forces surrounded the national university, locking hundreds of people inside.

Jan. 22 – Demonstrators from the group BPR reported that across the street from El Rosario, in Parque Libertad, they were sprayed with the insecticide malathion.

---

*

Mami enrolled Camila and me in swimming lessons. The pool was attached to a private gym a short walk from our house—we walked longer to get to school than to reach the gym. The pool was behind a metal gate easily mistaken for a car garage. It was surrounded by lush greenery and under the tropical sun it sparkled turquoise and gold. Our swimming instructor, a svelte middle-aged man, took his job seriously. He drilled us on proper technique relentlessly for fifty minutes, back and forth, back and forth the length of the pool but his sternness melted at the end of each lesson when he let us do what we most wanted: cannon ball, splash, and kick to oblivion.

We relished our swimming lessons but only when we were behind the metal gate. To get there Camila and I had to walk the length of the western side of a notorious garrison—Cuartel San Carlos. On our return home, full of chatter and lightness after playing in the water, we silenced ourselves the moment we turned the corner from the gym and faced the garrison's walls. We walked timorously alongside its exterior, topped with barbed wire, and tried to remain unimpressed with the turrets stationed with armed sentinels ready to discharge. My stomach turned into a knot whenever army trucks loaded with soldiers drove past us on the way to or from the garrison's main entrance. Only the sound of our flip-flops thwacking against our heels faster and faster could have betrayed our anxiety as we scurried like mice on our way home.

Jan. 23 – The military fence that prevented entry and exit to the university has been lifted. Students from the group the Unidad Revolucionaria told the press that 40,000 students, campesinos, and supporters trapped inside needed to return to their homes.

Jan 25 – Three thousand acres of sugar plantations were burned by the BPR in the north of the country.

We'd heard stories of soldiers who, jittery and mistrustful of guerrilla tactics, had discharged their weapons onto groups of innocent civilians. What if they discharged their guns on us? What if they were in a bad mood that afternoon? What if they noticed our comings and goings with bags bulging with wet towels and swimsuits and found us suspicious? What if they thought we were some kind of informants? What if, right leg, what if, left leg. We got through that way, the length of the long street.

*

Even with the escalating violence around us, some social expectations remained. I learned to embroider at school for instance—backstitch, chain stitch, satin stitch—it was part of the repertoire a "good" girl needed to master to become a "good" woman. By eighth grade the hope was that we would reach a degree of high efficacy with floss and needle. On one occasion the project was a tea towel. The craft teacher called us one by one to the front of the room to present our work. Up went the tall girl who sat behind me. She ensured, as she sauntered up to the teacher's desk, that her finished towel was visible, the cornucopia motif in the middle of her towel resplendent in bright, perfectly smooth, adroitly placed stitches. One after the other my classmates walked up to the desk, showing off projects that demonstrated effort and skill while, with ever-rising dread, I looked at the cloth crumpled at the bottom of my school bag, the edges of which embodied the word "ragged."

Jan. 25 – The Nicaraguan embassy was riddled with bullets.

Jan. 27 – In Coatepeque, 20 members of the FPL were killed after fighting with elements of the National Second Brigade.

My design was not only halfway finished; the stiches, pulled too tight here and there, gave my work a puckered effect. I prayed for something to deliver me from the inevitable embarrassment, like an earthquake, or maybe the teacher suffering a minor heart attack, nothing serious, one from which she'd recover quickly, but something, anything, because my work was looking to take the Worst in Class category by a landslide. Fretting in my seat, I missed when two men barged into our classroom. Men were a rare presence at Escuela España. We had one, maybe two, male teachers, but these men had their faces half covered with red handkerchiefs. They demanded that everyone, including our teacher, line up and come out to the yard, and it was clear by the tone of their voices that they were not to be disobeyed.

In Escuela España the lower grades were housed in the building's downstairs and the upper grades on the second floor. Camila was three years younger in age than me but four years behind me in school, which meant that her classroom was on the main floor. When we reached the downstairs lobby, all of the seventh-, eighth-, and ninth-grade students and their teachers were already waiting. There were a few other men with handkerchiefs on their faces and they led us past the front courtyard out to the least-used part of the school, the swimming pool, which for years sat abandoned, gathering trash and weeds. By the teachers and students gathered in the foyer, I saw that only second-floor classes had been disrupted. Camila was safe.

When people sympathized with individuals with kerchief-covered faces, they referred to them as "muchachos." Those who didn't called

February 1980

Feb. 4 – The organization LP-28 has occupied Spain's embassy. Dr. Victor Sánchez Meza, its ambassador, is inside the premises.

Feb. 4 – The church El Rosario in San Salvador was sprayed with gunfire from a moving vehicle, killing three and injuring many of the people who were taking refuge there.

---

them "insurgentes." At that moment it didn't matter what sympathies or objections anyone had. The looks on the teachers' faces mirrored our fears and concerns. The eight to ten men commanded us to line up along the edge of the pool. In our white uniforms and tall white socks, we were a guirnalda de palomitas de maíz, a garland of popcorn doves. The leader of the troop spoke with conviction about how the "landowner dogs," "los perros terratenientes," working with their "armed dogs" and "puppet government dogs," oppressed us, the people. "¡Revolución o Muerte! ¡Hasta la Victoria!"

Another man took center stage and proceeded with a lesson on how to make a Molotov cocktail. The man was clearly nervous and almost dropped the soda bottle he was using for the demonstration. He showed us each step haphazardly—this was no hands-on, careful science lesson—his hands and mouth appeared disconnected from each other as he poured gasoline into the bottle and talked about why these type of weapons were important to us, and how we, "the people," could use them to inflict damage on all the dogs. I had seen the damage the bombs could inflict. Days earlier I'd witnessed a bus set on fire in the middle of a street near the school. I'd walked past the stench of rubber, watched the flames devour the bus's interior, charring metal and melting the upholstery, seen plumes of black smoke escaping through the open windows. I knew the bus had not been set on fire by police or soldiers, but by people who covered half their faces with handkerchiefs so that when they threw Molotov cocktails they could not be easily identified.

Feb. 5 – Mario Aguiñada Carranza and Norma Guevara, members of the leftist organization UDN, have disappeared.

Feb. 8 – Roberto D'Aubuisson, in a television special, denounced an international communist conspiracy in El Salvador.

We stood around the edge of the empty pool, terrified on the inside, but stoic on the outside. Everyone—teachers and students—knew that if an army convoy, a military jeep, or la Policía Nacional, all of whom patrolled city streets, caught sight of us, this would most likely be our last lesson. The guerrillas knew this too and infused their speech with a combination of defiance, haste, and fear. They were visibly shaken. When the presentation ended, the men, like wayward spirits, disappeared into the school grounds, each following a separate exit route. We walked back to the main building huddled in our friend groups. The teachers walked together and spoke with one another in hushed tones. We didn't go back to our sewing examination. Matters of cornucopias and bright embroidery floss felt irrelevant. The season of carefree domesticity, or the hope for it implicit in our assignment, now belonged to another time.

*

And so it was that, another time, I found myself on my own with only Reina in the house. From our house's upstairs corridor, I could see her bent over the large cement washbasin, scrubbing the day's laundry. Frederick slept curled up on Camila's bed and Monina napped on the patio tiles, still cool from the previous night. Drawn by curiosity I peeked inside Tío Javier and Mónica's room, which was off-limits to Camila and me. The largest of the bedrooms, it had its own balcony, and in the morning's solitude, it felt more like a den, the drawn curtains adding a touch of erotic mystery. No one spoke of it, I had

---

Feb. 12 – Six dead after the offices of the PDC were forcibly emptied.
Feb. 14 – Goldtree, a store in San Miguel, was burned before a standoff between militants and government armed forces.

Feb. 19 – In Zaragoza three children ages 8, 10, and 17 were killed while carrying a bomb they thought was a refrigerator replacement piece.

---

not heard any of the tías mention it, but Tío Javier and Mónica were living together without matrimony. That gave Mónica a dangerous allure. She was doing what movie heroines did.

I slid open the closet door and slipped on a pair of Mónica's high-heeled sandals, hoping that some of her glamour would rub off on me. Unsteady on my feet, I paraded about, looking at my reflection in the room's full-length mirror. Mónica had several pairs of strappy sandals, some with higher heels than others. I tried them all, admiring my figure on the wall mirror. Hours passed. I bent to strap on the last pair and that's when I saw it. How I had missed it earlier, I could not tell, but there, taped to the narrow door that led to the balcony, was a black-and-white poster of Edén Pastora, Comandante Cero, the Nicaraguan Sandinista revolutionary, looking straight at me, a beret angled on his head, and the cannon of a rifle framing the right-hand side of his handsome face. I dared him, standing tall in my borrowed heels, feeling defiance rising in me. My brio was soon deflated, however, when I realized that if our house were searched by police forces at that moment—searches were a common occurrence—the poster would implicate us. Tío Javier and Papá would be taken away. Mami and Mónica would most likely also be taken away to wherever people were dragged to, to be tortured and possibly never to be seen again. Camila and me? Reina? Would we be taken?

*

Feb. 20 – A powerful bomb caused severe damage to the Jesuit University of Central America and destroyed the radio station YSAX.

Feb. 22 – Cayetano Carpio, leader of the group FPL, stated in an interview conducted by the Mexican newspaper *El Excélsior* that "the popular revolutionary government would put an end to the dominance of the fourteen families and the guardians of their riches, and it would not be socialist in character."

I was aware that Tía Maura had applied to the US government for our visas but that didn't guarantee anything. The possibility that permission to immigrate would be granted was a slim one, but worth trying, Mami said. Tía Maura agreed. Papá did not disagree but neither did he embrace the idea. In 1979 leaving the country was something few imagined or even desired—unless a person was very wealthy or a university student needing to study abroad, no one talked about leaving. My parents lacked a full understanding about the process and its expense, our prospects appeared bleak, but they were clear about the stakes. It was a matter of life and death.

In San Salvador, we spent more time with Tía Dalia and her family. Tía Dalia was the fourth born of Mami's nine siblings. When we lived in Atiquizaya she and her children were our distant relatives, but now we saw one another almost every weekend. Tía Dalia had an older daughter, Carola, and three younger children who were closer in age to me and my sister. Carola was eighteen at the time and had started dating. Yuri and Glenda sometimes teased each other about a neighborhood boy they liked but I never saw them walking or holding hands with anyone. Ana, Tía Salma's oldest daughter, had a boyfriend who came over every night punctually at 7 P.M. and sat with her, sometimes holding her hand, on the front steps until Abue shouted from the living room into the darkness, "It's nine o'clock!" Abue was so punctual with her call that if several of us cousins were over at their house, we would mouth Abue's admonishment in jest and peek through the living room window to see Ana's annoyed

Feb. 22 – FENASTRAS is calling for a general strike.
Feb. 27 – The United States has begun to disburse $50 million to the Revolutionary Government of El Salvador as emergency aid.

March 1980
Mar. 4 – Buses and tires left to burn across intersections.

reaction. We knew Abue's call grated on her. Every night a delight and a slight awaited her on the front steps of their house.

One afternoon while I was over at Tía Dalia's house one of Carola's suitors paid her a visit. The boyfriend visit routine was the same in all the households: After a general greeting and short chat with the adults in the family, the couple was left alone for an hour or two in an open part of the house. It was understood that no one should bother the pair while the visit lasted. Carola and her suitor sat demurely, with a respectful space between them, on the living room sofa. Knowing that I would not be welcome in their space once they started talking, I scurried to get snacks from the kitchen. On my way back to the bedroom where all of us younger cousins had gathered, I managed to get a good look at the two of them. He was much older than her and worked hard to show whatever measure of his teenager self was left in his twenty-something body. But she possessed an uncanny precision in her actions and managed to be measured and spontaneous, coquettish and demure, in order to convey a persona older than her years. His face was turned to hers and his thick mustache stretched wide over his upper lip. The rolled-up sleeves of his creased button-down shirt revealed a thick mat covering his forearms. I could tell that if he were to leave the top eyelets of his shirt unbuttoned, his chest would be a dark follicular extravaganza. I knew this because Señor Maravilla, my sixth- and seventh-grade language teacher, left the top buttons of his shirts open, á la John Travolta in *Saturday Night Fever*, to showcase his chest hair. I was a good student, took notes dutifully,

Mar. 6 – The government declares state of emergency across the country.
Mar. 9 – Eleven dead in San Miguel after an encounter between army troops and members of MERS and BPR inside the secondary school Instituto Nacional Isidro Menéndez.

Mar. 10 – Three children dead in Colonia IVU after touching a bomb abandoned in a trash pile.

and paid attention to the contours of his face, the line of his jaw, the shape of his neck, and his thickly matted chest.

Coming back from the kitchen, through the open living area, my pockets stuffed with galletas, I saw, sticking out from under the visitor's thigh, a metralleta. Carola sat closer to the wall and was at that moment smiling, saying something in hushed tones that forced him to lean in her direction, thereby lifting his thigh and revealing the weapon. My heart racing, I made a beeline to the bedroom where my sister and my younger cousins awaited the snacks. I intuited a few things about this man with the thick mustache and the Sirocco parked outside. I intuited that he must fear a guerrilla ambush to carry the gun inside the house to court a beautiful girl.

It crossed my mind that he probably knew military henchmen. Maybe he was someone to be feared. Maybe he hunted down teachers like Señor Cabrera. Maybe he did not hunt down teachers himself, maybe he gave orders to have others kill them. I intuited that this mustachioed man would not be one of my parents' friends. No, he would not be. But I feared that he could be their killer.

Mar. 13 – In San Salvador, a dynamite explosion damaged the Human Rights Commission building, and a second bomb exploded in the building that housed the newspaper *El Independiente*.

12

One Stitch at a Time

Oakland, California, 2004

"I made an appointment to see Noreen next week," I said to John as casually as I could while stirring a pot of black beans on the stove. I was trying a new recipe, adding fresh cilantro to the pot as the beans cooked, and the smell was enticing.

"I have a feeling you'll like working with her. Charles could not stop singing her praises," he said, while pulling out bowls from the cupboard to set the dinner table. Baby Izal bounced in his chair. Aurora tried to ignore him, playing with her dolls in the dining room. Toby would have normally been sniffing around, but a few weeks earlier we'd given him to a local pug rescue organization after he bit Aurora on the cheek a second time. She liked to crawl into his basket and he defended his turf. It was sad to let him go but the vet was uncompromising. She was right. We could not have a dog at home prone to biting our toddler.

"Did you get a chance to look at the listings?" I asked, knowing he probably hadn't. He was not interested in moving. To his credit John had been forthright about it all along and told me so a thousand times. His mantra: Nowhere will we find a house with a location as great as this one, close to downtown Berkeley and Oakland, with a yard as big as the one we had, with neighbors as nice as the ones we had, as affordable as the one we had.

"You know, even if we sell this house well, we couldn't buy a house with all the things you want and still keep a mortgage as comfortable as the one we have now," he said.

"But, John, everyone we know who own homes are managing mortgages much, much, higher than ours. We can do it. I know we can." I insisted. By now John was washing the rice for our rice-and-bean-bowl dinner. I'd moved onto making a fresh salsa.

"Well, I did look at the packet," he said, "and saw a couple of houses closer to Lake Merritt that look interesting . . ."

"Would you be okay with me contacting the realtor, asking her to show us the properties?" I asked. After a long pause he agreed.

Meanwhile, I held up my side of the deal and reached out to the therapist. Noreen saw patients in a nondescript craftsman bungalow on the small commercial strip of the Glenview neighborhood, a block south of a quaint hardware store, a cleaners, a small grocer, two restaurants, and a coffee shop. The door of the house was always unlocked, and the small living room had a few chairs and piles of up-to-date magazines to distract patients from the fact that at that very moment they were there because their lives were fraying at the edges.

That first visit, I protested and cursed the entire drive from downtown, where I worked, to this hilly part of the city: *What am I doing? Do I really need this? Is this really a good use of my time?* In the dark paneled room, I pretended to browse the magazines, but kept my eye on the only other door in the room, the one that led to one's ravaged interior. A light turned green next to Noreen's name and soon after the door opened and a middle-aged woman with a head of tight brown and graying curls stuck her head into the waiting room.

"Claudia?" she asked.

I followed her down a short corridor and into the first door on the right. In the house's earlier life, this must have been a bedroom. A west-facing double-hung window let light pour into the room and gather on the brown coffee table upon which rested a woven basket and a box of Kleenex. Behind the table was a chocolate leather sofa with end tables and more Kleenex boxes.

Noreen's desk was tucked to the right of the window. She motioned for me to take the sofa; she sat on her chair and swiveled to face me. She had a soothing presence. Her chestnut hair framed her fair face in a gentle way, and her brown eyes were inquisitive and warm. Everything about her demeanor, from her slacks and blazer to her unmanicured nails, to the way she leaned forward, said that she was there to listen. I liked all of that, but I was reticent. I was not going to give an inch, still feeling the burn from the previous therapist.

"Tell me about yourself," Noreen said. "What brings you here?"

This time I started with the shooting in front of the house and related the event with as much detail as I could, leaving out the connection to El Salvador, though I did mention in my introduction that I was originally from there. She leaned in and looked at me intently the entire time I spoke. When I was done, she sat up, leaned in even more and asked:

"And . . . does any of this remind you of your life in El Salvador?"

I didn't see the question coming. We both knew what she meant by "any of this." She meant shootings, government repression, killings, kidnappings, terror. No one I had ever met had made the connection so quickly between my state of being and my personal history. I had never quite articulated to myself that what we lived through in El Salvador had injured us deeply enough to influence our lives decades later.

Back then the word "trauma" did not exist in my vocabulary, nor in my parents', nor in the lexicon of anyone I knew. In my mind, the word "trauma" belonged to military personnel, not to private citizens. I had never imagined that it could apply to my family. Until my visit to Noreen, I had never fully attempted to use such words, to reach for language to name the things that formed our experience. History happened. There was a war. People we knew were murdered, tortured. They fled as we ourselves fled, but we never insisted on the subjectivity of our experiences. We folded ourselves against the historical backdrop. We were but a few among thousands of others faceless casualties of the violence. Our existence had, until then, been as if we were ahistorical beings. Surviving required us to exist in a kind of fog. There was simply no time, space, or energy left at the end of the day to consider the ways in which we were war casualties.

That night, reading a bedtime story to Aurora, I was overcome with emotion. I choked back tears and stumbled through the words.

"What's wrong, Mami? Are you okay?" Aurora asked, looking at me intently from under the covers.

"I am fine, sweetie," I lied. "The story somehow made me sad, that is all." I tucked her into a tamalito—our bedtime game of folding the sheets tightly around her to make her resemble a tamale. I turned off the lights and walked out of her bedroom knowing that I was not at all okay. And I didn't know what would make things better.

13

Dancing in the Time of War

San Salvador, El Salvador, 1980

The midday heat of March and April assaults skin and mind alike. It can thrust anyone into a state of desperation. Desperation is also what we felt hearing constant shootings, sometimes near, sometimes far away. This morning, every intersection leading into our colonia was blocked off. Cuartel San Carlos, close to our house, must have been on hyper alert as they set up barricades around our colonia. No one could leave and no one could come into the neighborhood. Still, Tío Javier dressed for work.

"¡Javier, no podés ir, hombre!" Mami's shaky voice said.

"Pero me llamaron del hospital. Ha de estar fea la cosa. Tengo que ir." They need people at the hospital, my uncle said.

Mar. 17 – Bombs exploded in the offices of the Ministry of Agriculture in San Salvador, Zacatecoluca, Ahuachapán, and San Miguel.
Mar. 17 – A public transport stoppage had been declared in San Salvador and Santa Ana.

Mar. 24 – Inside the chapel of the hospital la Divina Providencia in Colonia Miramonte, Monseñor Óscar Arnulfo Romero was killed while celebrating mass. A few days earlier he had criticized the levels of violence directed at urban workers and campesinos and said that 150 individuals had been killed from the 16th to the 22nd of March.

"¡Te pueden matar!"—You could be killed! Mami said, raising her voice.

"Pues si me matan, que me maten," Tío Javier said. If they kill me, they kill me. He headed out the door. If the hospital had summoned him, the situation must have been bad, he'd said, and as an operating room physician he felt the obligation to go. From my upstairs window I watched his figure walking toward the armed blockade. He took large steps. He wore khaki pants and a cream polo shirt, the palms of his hands open at his sides.

The war we lived made people do the unthinkable. Papá, who all my life had opposed anything and everything to do with the church and organized religion, now tuned on his transistor radio to hear Monseñor Romero deliver his Sunday homilies. This gesture was a far cry from when he castigated Abuela for taking me to a late afternoon mass. In Colonia San Carlos, Mami, Papá, Tío Javier, Mónica, Camila, Reina, I, and sometimes even Monina, huddled on the stairs leading up to the second floor to hear Monseñor's voice rise and fill the air with urgency and hope, and we clung to his every word. Unafraid, he recounted the violence in our cities and rural villages. He remembered and honored the innocent killed. He implored la policía, el ejército, los escuadrones to end the violence. Urgently, he demanded a stop to the killings. He ordered a direct cease to the widespread repression. Monseñor was the only person in the country with the moral and spiritual authority to make such public demands. We kept the radio's volume low. We didn't want anyone passing by our house to hear Monseñor's voice and label us as "sympathizers."

Mar. 30 – Violent disturbances broke out while the funeral of Monseñor Óscar Arnulfo Romero was underway. According to witnesses, the unrest was triggered by the detonation of a bomb in the square facing the cathedral.

Mar. 30 – The crowd, estimated at 50,000 people, was gripped by panic. Several businesses were looted—resulting in losses amounting to thousands of colones—and vehicles were set on fire.

At thirteen I understood that to call out injustice and repression, to speak against the military, was to risk your life, and it was clear that Monseñor risked his often.

One day while Mami and Papá were still at work, Reina and I went to the local supermarket on foot. The store was a few blocks away from the house. Camila, then ten years old, chose to stay home. "I'll be fine," she told us. "You'll be right back." It was late afternoon; dust swirled about on streets and sidewalks as rush-hour traffic drove past and students, wearing various uniforms, hurried home after a long day at school.

The shots rang out loudly. Nearby. Like everyone else, we panicked and rushed inside the store. People huddled screaming, shaking, mumbling Hail Marys and Padre Nuestros. The store employees immediately locked up and we waited out the gunfire. When we arrived home Camila's eyes were swollen. We took too long, she explained, the shots went on and on and she didn't know what else to do. She was standing next to the credenza with a pair of scissors in front of her, locks of hair scattered on the tile floor. I stared at her, guilt spreading over my body for having left her alone. I could not find any words inside myself to make her feel better. Reina got down on one knee and held her in a long embrace.

Then Tío Javier and Mónica decided to formally start a life together and rented a house on their own. It was a sad moment. We had learned to live with one another and enjoy one another's company. Miralvalle, our new colonia, was a hilly place, and back then there were still sylvan pockets of undeveloped land around it. Despite

---

Mar. 30 – The latest report states that 27 people were killed and more than 200 injured.

April 1980
Apr. 1 – On this day several bombs exploded in neighborhoods around San Salvador including: Escalón, San Benito, Concepción, and San Jacinto.

---

missing Tío Javier and Mónica our move was not all bad; Tía Dalia, Carola's mother, lived mere blocks away. Our houses were located on the same street; Tía's was located on a cul-de-sac at the bottom of a long hill whereas ours was at the top of the rise. I took full advantage of the slope to teach myself to ride my bike downhill without using the handlebars. I'd push off at the top of the street, lean back on the banana seat, and swoosh, the handlebar streamers flayed backward, dust and hot air swirled around my face, and my body swelled with a feeling of flying, like I imagined freedom to be.

The new house, like our previous one in Colonia San Carlos, had two stories. The first floor fit only three smallish rooms, but the upstairs was wedged against a rising slope and had generous bedrooms, a large, grassy area, and an expansive terrace overlooking the city center in the valley below. On the lawn I spent hours sketching, with great anatomical detail, whatever insects and grubs I could find. *This is what explorers do*, I told myself: *record their world*. From my bedroom window, and sometimes from the large balcony, I watched the city succumb to evening, lights slowly coming on, then sparkling. It was a loveliness, to witness the day's surrender amidst the violence that short circuited our every day.

One afternoon the slow churning of wheels in front of our house jarred me into alertness as I lay on my bed daydreaming of a boy I had recently met. A rusty white pickup was driving away from the corner where we lived. Minutes later it returned. From my bedroom window I could see the driver in the cabin and a second young man crouching in the bed of the pickup truck. The young man in the

---

Apr. 9 – Twenty-five campesinos were killed near the rural area Monte de San Juan, Cuscatlán.

Apr. 14 – The mayor of Soyapango, José Atilio Estrada Machuca, was killed in city hall by members of the FPL.

back jumped out and stealthily ran up to the corner house while the truck drove away. From a crossbody bag he pulled a spray can and began tagging the wall. He worked fast, taking quick side glances as he went. The afternoon sun illuminated his profile. From my angle I could not see what he was writing, but I had an inkling. The city had innumerable tags that represented political groups' acronyms or that read along the same lines: "BPR Hasta la Victoria Siempre," "Patria o Muerte," "Basta la represión contra el pueblo."

At around the same time we moved to Colonia Miralvalle, a series of television and radio commercials flooded the airwaves, encouraging listeners and viewers to help combat "subversives." The baritone voice gave out a telephone number to call in case one saw or suspected any type of subversive activity. The ads didn't specify what activities fell under the subversive category, nor whose interests the voice represented; this was left to the inference of the viewer or listener. The voice said things along the lines of "Patriots! Report subversives," and then enunciated each digit in the hotline's telephone number.

The pickup pulled up again in front of the house and the young man threw himself in the bed. A few minutes later, I heard the shots. They were loud, nearby. I wondered if someone who had seen what I witnessed had called the flashing number on the TV screen. The number we had probably all unwittingly or willingly memorized. Sitting on my bed, over the pink coverlet, in the security of my room, I figured that one of the young men, or both, had been killed. Immediately, Reina appeared at the entrance of my room, "¿Niña, oyó los tiros?"

Apr. 17 – The mayor of Quezaltepeque, Prof. Rodolfo Antonio Chamorro García, was killed.

Apr. 18 – The bodies of five youths shot to death were found in various parts of San Salvador.

"Sí, Reina," I said. I had heard the shots. She seemed agitated and excited at the same time.

"¿Vamos a ver?" she asked.

"No," I said. I did not want to check out what had happened.

A couple of months before that fateful afternoon, Mami had come home to tell me with rousing excitement that Doña Alejandra's twins were having a quinceañera and wanted me to join their court of honor.

"¡Por favor, no, Mami!" I pleaded—to put on a formal dress, enter church on the arm of a young man for a Te Deum mass, and dance a waltz in front of hundreds in the arms of an eager teenage boy was the last thing I desired.

"¡No Mami, no quiero," I pleaded, "Por favor, don't make me do it!"

"No te preocupes," Mami said. "Alejandra told me she found the nicest young man to be your partner. You will enjoy yourself; you'll see."

I went to the first rehearsal anticipating a catastrophe. I didn't like the pomp and circumstance of quinceañeras; I thought them a waste of energy and money. When I arrived at the dance studio the family had rented to practice the waltz we would be performing at the event, the twins greeted me joyously, as did Doña Alejandra, who was one of Mami's oldest friends. She motioned for me to come, she wanted to introduce me to . . . "¡Jorge!" she said, in the direction of the crowd of boys goofing off in a corner. A tall, slender, blond boy raised his head and walked in our direction. All I could think to myself was how on earth had I ended up being paired up with the one blond boy in the room? Surely a snob, I told myself. Before I could fake

Apr. 18 – A bomb exploded in the offices of the newspaper *La Crónica del Pueblo*.

Apr. 21 – The bodies of eight people were found shot to death in Santiago de María.

a headache to excuse myself from the entire enterprise, the pleasant looking Jorge was standing in front of me, offering his hand with an affable smile rippling across his face. The rehearsal ended sooner than I imagined. It turned out Jorge, like me, had no clue about waltzes and Te Deums, and, like me, had been forced by his mother to be part of the twins' court.

The first rehearsals were awkward, but pleasant. As the weeks went by I found myself looking forward to them, looking forward to Jorge's hand around my waist, to his jokes and genuine smile. He was clearly pleased to see me every time. He held my hand with tenderness as we walked to our place on the dance floor. After weeks of rehearsals the day for the quinceañera arrived. Early in the day Mami took me to a salon to get my hair washed and blow-dried, and while she and Papá put on their fine clothes, I fidgeted in my room with the spaghetti straps of the blue-and-white taffeta gown the girls in the court would wear. Camila helped me fasten the heeled sandals Mami bought me for the occasion. Once ready, I was transformed, toda una señorita.

Jorge was already there when we arrived at the park next to the church where the court gathered for photographs before mass. My heart leapt when I saw him in the crowd with the other pages all smartly dressed in blue suits. He looked smashing, his hair neatly combed to one side, his body slender and strong. I wanted nothing more than to be alone with him, to feel his body close to mine, to feel what it was like to be kissed. The celebration was a success. The twins were happy. Doña Alejandra and her husband were happy. I

Apr. 28 – Mr. Victor Keilhauer is kidnapped in front of his business on Boulevard del Ejército, San Salvador. No one took responsibility.

May 1980
May 6 – Eight bodies were found in different parts of San Salvador. El Escuadrón de la Muerte, the death squads, took responsibility for five of them.

---

was happy. Jorge was happy. The reception was held in a circular space with open walls surrounded by gardens, clearly landscaped for special occasions. Tables were arranged along the outside of the circle, leaving the middle as a large dance floor. Jorge and I waltzed in front of the huge crowd in our formal attire, synchronizing without fault. After the meal, when the music turned to popular tunes, we danced solely with each other with abandon. At one point we held hands and walked away from the illuminated space and into the gardens. I looked back toward the party and caught sight of Mami, who sat cross-legged, with a drink in her hand, laughing with Doña Alejandra, who sat across from her. Mami was thoroughly enjoying herself. It had been a long time since I last saw her relaxed and laughing.

At the end of the evening, Jorge told me he wanted me to be his girlfriend. I wanted to be his girlfriend too. But I was afraid my parents would disapprove. I was too young, they would say, I knew it. Besides, Jorge and I lived and went to school on opposite sides of the city and the situation was such that neither he nor I could sneak after school to meet in a movie theater or in a park to hold hands and steal a kiss. The odds were strong against us. He asked for my phone number instead and said that we could at least talk to each other. In the days following the party, I both dreaded and dreamt of his phone call. I didn't want to hear my parents' disapproval when they found out I was talking with a boy, but I longed to stay in touch with Jorge, to hear his voice, laugh with him. In fact, I was dreaming of his voice when the sound of the pickup truck circling our block woke me from my reverie.

May 7 – Captured in Santa Tecla, Mayor Roberto D'Aubuisson, eight army officers, and various civilians were taken to Cuartel San Carlos, where they remained accused of conspiracy to topple the current Government Junta.

May 9 – In Zacatecoluca, five students were abducted and later killed.

"Spirits dance in treetops," my Tía Valeria had once told me. If the spirit is a bad one, and is living in a backyard tree, you might as well chop the tree down. She had done just that with a regal sour orange tree, to Papá's dismay. When we left Atiquizaya for Santa Ana, Abuela and Tía Valeria bought our house and moved in. For years Papá had cared for the tree, planting his rose garden underneath it to shade his beloved flowers from the scorching sun. Tía determined that a bad spirit had settled there and that the tree needed to come down.

The afternoon of the pickup truck incident, after the echo of the shots subsided, looking out my window at the city, I took solace in the knowledge my aunt had shared with me. If the young men had indeed been killed, then their souls had plenty of trees to choose to inhabit in the hills behind our colonia. Maybe that is how spirits seized the trees in the first place, their souls fresh off the bone, escaping a body still half attached to the living. As poltergeists inhabiting the geometry of a tree canopy, spirits may yet fool death. To be forgotten is to be truly dead, but birds live in trees, and they can sense ghosts' prophetic acrobatics, hear the shades of their laments, smeared like sunlight on trembling leaves.

A few weeks after the tagging incident, Mami rushed into the house breathing hard, as if she had run nonstop from the bus stop and up the hilly blocks to our house. Once inside, she quickly shut the door behind her. I looked at her from my spot on the living room sofa and Reina, responding to the door's thud, stepped into the living room from the kitchen, where she was preparing the evening's meal.

"¡Lo mataron!" Mami said. First looking at Reina, then at me.

May 9 – As a reaction to the murder of ANDES (Association of Salvadoran Educators) leader Héctor Ramón Guardado, people sat en masse in the following Catholic churches in San Salvador: El Rosario, Don Rúa, El Calvario, Concepción, the Cathedral, and the church in Antiguo Cuscatlán.

May 12 – Death squads demanded the release of Mayor D'Aubuisson and all others detained. They threaten to dynamite radio stations and newspaper offices, including those of *La Prensa Grâfica* in El Salvador, Guatemala, and Honduras, unless their demands are met by next Monday.

"Lo mataron mientras daba misa en una capilla. Lo anunciaron por los altoparlantes en la U." Though she didn't utter his name, we knew she meant Monseñor Romero. He'd been assassinated.

"¡Ay Dios Santo! ¡Doña Inez!" exclaimed Reina, clasping her hands to her chest.

Mayhem broke out like wildfire when his death was announced through the university loudspeakers, Mami said, still standing a few steps from the front door. She told us about how everyone ran out of classrooms, toppling desks, scrambling over one another, crying and screaming while the loudspeakers encouraged everyone to immediately evacuate the university premises. Monseñor Romero had been killed while officiating mass and there was reason to think that the university, and other places around the country, could face attacks from the government's armed forces.

Mami spoke as a somnambulist might, not quite knowing or believing what she had just related, confused about what to do next. "I could not find your papá," she said, looking squarely at me. "I decided to rush here instead. We all ran away before the army showed up. We were certain they were coming," she said. Speechless, I looked at Mami, who by now was looking again at Reina, who stared back at her. We went quiet, our silence interrupted by the sizzle of the evening plantains frying in the kitchen.

During the final weeks of Lent, Catholic churches cover crucifixes, saints, and sacred images with a black shroud, finally removing the coverings at the beginning of Easter Vigil Mass in anticipation of Christ's resurrection and the return of the light at Easter. It is striking

May 16 – Fifteen dead in San Miguel due to violence.

May 22 – In Santa Ana Ronald Judá Muller Argumendo was assassinated in his home by unknown armed individuals. He had recently graduated with a degree in social science from the University of El Salvador.

---

to see the arrested statues, their fields of vision negated. They see nothing, they hear nothing, they speak nothing. The days following Monseñor's assassination were like that. We lived, somehow, but were shrouded in darkness. It was impossible to think what would happen next, or rather, we knew what would happen next and were too afraid to put it into words. As a thirteen-year-old I understood clearly that my family, my cousins, tías, tíos, teachers, classmates, all of us were inconsequential. He had been a shield. Whatever barrier he mustered to protect us disappeared with his last breath.

Monseñor's body was held in state in the Metropolitan Cathedral in San Salvador. Thousands of people from all over the country came to pay their last respects. They started arriving a few days before the funeral mass and came crammed on buses, squeezed on the back of pickup trucks. Papá said he wanted to attend the funeral procession, but Mami begged him not to go; she had a premonition that things would go badly, she said. No one spoke things directly anymore, even in the privacy of our own homes. What Mami meant to say was that she feared there would be a massacre.

The Sunday Monseñor was laid to rest opened with the roar of helicopters. The hills of Colonia Miralvalle offered us a good vantage point and from our balcony we saw choppers over the city center. Sometimes their sound reached us clearly as they ventured in our direction. Mami could not stop running to the bathroom. My throat fluttered like I had a bird trapped inside. I moved from one room to the next, from the upstairs balcony to the kitchen downstairs, back upstairs to my room, repeating under my breath what had become a

---

May 26 – A teacher, José Francisco Melara González, was machine-gunned down in San Antonio Abad. He was principal of the school Escuela Rural Mixta "Juana López." The crime was carried out by individuals in a car.

May 29 – After his house was searched, the former minister of education, Licenciado Salvador Ricardo Samayoa Leiva, was abducted. He belonged to the leftist organization FPL.

---

kind of salvo: "Please let there be no massacre, please let there be no massacre." From our balcony we watched the city and imagined the scene on the ground. The next day the newspapers carried images of the streets around the cathedral littered with hundreds of shoes that had been left behind when the crowd panicked and ran desperately seeking safety as gunfire tore through the solemn moment.

As an adult I have sat with the photographs of Monseñor's burial mass many times. Reports of the number of people in attendance vary, but most news accounts list between one hundred thousand and one hundred and fifty thousand individuals present. The tension was extreme but the need to honor and mourn Monseñor overpowered fears. The crowd spilled onto Parque Libertad and the streets surrounding the cathedral. Shots were fired from the rooftops of adjacent buildings. Smoke bombs detonated. At the sound of gunfire everyone hustled for cover, behind cars, in the park, crouching behind any low wall, and running away as fast and far as possible. The photographs of the aftermath show the wreckage: desolate streets strewn with shoes, crumpled signs and, like rising smoke after a fire, the terror of thousands of bodies who had risked their lives to say "¡Presente!" The figures of the dead and wounded also vary; one newspaper reported twenty-seven people dead and two hundred wounded. But I have read of up to forty dead and two hundred wounded. My reaction to the photographs is the same every time: disbelief and awe at the bravery and faith of my compatriots.

May 30 – The lawyer Dr. Juan José Rugamas was assassinated in his home. The crime was claimed by members of the ERP.

June 1980

June 5 – Teacher Jose Mauricio Flores died hours after being riddled with bullets near the school where he worked.

June 14 – The priest Francisco Cossme Spesotte, Episcopal Vicar, was riddled with bullets inside the church Parroquial de San Juan Nonualco in La Paz.

Violence was a fire which swept over the fields of El Salvador; it burst into villages, cut off roads and destroyed highways and bridges, energy sources and transmission lines; it reached the cities and entered families, sacred areas and educational centers; it struck at justice and filled the public administration with victims; and it singled out as an enemy anyone who was not on the list of friends. Violence turned everything to death and destruction, for such is the senselessness of that breach of the calm plenitude which accompanies the rule of law, the essential nature of violence being suddenly or gradually to alter the certainty which the law nurtures in human beings when this change does not take place through the normal mechanisms of the rule of law. The victims were Salvadorians and foreigners of all backgrounds and all social and economic classes, for in its blind cruelty violence leaves everyone equally defenseless.

—United Nations Commission on the Truth for El Salvador, *From Madness to Hope: The 12-Year War in El Salvador; Report of the Commission on the Truth for El Salvador* (1993)

June 24 – Eight people killed— among them, two doctors, two medical students, and a nurse—during a shootout that happened when government forces searched a house in Colonia Santa Lucía in Santa Ana.

14

Diagnosis

Oakland, California, 2004

My visits to Noreen shaped into a pattern: On the day of our appointment, I'd leave work early and drive toward the city's hills, the entire way telling myself I had nothing to share. From whichever spot I parked the car, like a reprimanded kid, I dragged my feet, kicked a stone or two, cursed out John, mumbled the reasons why this was a waste of time—and money—all the way up the steps that led me to the nondescript brown house and to the leather sofa across from the woman with chestnut hair who, for an hour, listened to me intently.

I started therapy with mistrust but as I opened up to Noreen more and more over time my eagerness to have these conversations began to reshape my visits. I had never engaged in the same way with another person. Noreen was a stranger, yet I shared my personal life with her and in the process discovered motives behind windows I did not know I possessed. When each session was over, after I'd spewed forth a torrent of words, I left through the back door, clutching spent Kleenexes, exhausted yet lighter. I'd slip on sunglasses at a time when the sun was setting to spare anyone the spectacle of my swollen eyes. The rear door existed to let all the blessed souls reduced to pulp sitting on leather sofas behind closed doors have a measure of decorum when they exited with faces deformed by whatever rages, fears, epiphanies, and shames they had processed during their therapy session.

"This," Noreen said on a visit after we had established good rapport, "is the *DSM*. I want to read you the definition of post-traumatic stress disorder." Before I could object or offer an opinion, she launched into the reading. She read nonstop through the entire symptoms list. I sat across from her on the brown sofa sweating and cold at the same time. I couldn't hold on to the list of symptoms and behaviors. The words came at me rapid-fire; some ricocheted before I could parse out their meaning, but others bored right into me.

Witness Death Vigilance Flashbacks

Recurrent Startle Violent

Nightmare Death Witness

Distress Flashbacks Violent Avoidance

Recurrent Vigilance Startle

When she was done reading, Noreen lowered the thick volume, raised her eyes, and stared at me.

"Do you recognize any of those symptoms in yourself?" she asked.

I stared back, trying not to lose composure. As she'd read, I'd perceived items on the list like tree trunks in the forest I'd been lost in for years.

The words that had pierced me now throbbed. Each one was not just a word on its own but a link to a memory, a story, a fear, a loneliness. I couldn't fully hear what Noreen had read because the memories and feelings of my long-ago younger self were summoned so quickly by these words. Like thick graffiti on a wall on the side of a busy road, the words echoed inside me, along with their associations—a noisy roar, a complicated blur.

I had always thought that PTSD belonged to soldiers returning from war. To the veterans coming back from Iraq at the time. It belonged to rape survivors. It belonged to torture victims. Not to me, nor to my family. It lived far, far away from my everyday world. It haunted and harmed folks who had been through what I understood to be terrible trauma. Noreen, in her dark slacks, sat across from me with her legs crossed at her knee. The *DSM* rested on her lap, the page suspended by her right finger, as if to say, *If you don't believe me, I can read the list over again.*

15

Todos Contra Todos

San Salvador, El Salvador, 1980

A few weeks after Monseñor Romero's funeral mass, two well-mannered, well-dressed men came looking for Mami. I opened our front door with Reina behind me to find the two of them offering polite afternoon greetings. "Buenas tardes," the two men said in unison. They looked the way Papá did on any workday: short-sleeve button-down shirts with pens and small notebooks in their left pockets, dark slacks perfectly creased down the middle, and lace-up shoes. The short one with the clipboard asked: "Dispense, ¿aquí vive la señora Inez de Castro?"

Reina, standing right behind me, motioned her body forward, but before she could say a word, I blurted out, "Sí. Aquí vive," and without bothering to look back at her, I added, "But she is not here right now. She's at work . . . not at work, she . . . she is at the sewing

---

June 25 – Mechanic Armando Ramos killed by unknown men in his house in front of his family.
June 26 – Eleven people were assassinated on a soccer field by armed individuals, who shot straight into their faces. The victims were from Hacienda Proyecto San Antonio, Department of San Vicente.

July 1980
July 1 – Bombs damage businesses in Colonia Escálon and Colonia Roma in San Salvador.

school." Mami had recently started learning how to sew and attended classes at a sewing school in our colonia.

The men looked at each other. The taller one asked, "But . . . she does work at Alberto Masferrer School, no?" His voice was gentle. Even though I could feel Reina's bristling behind me, once more I confirmed their inquiry: "Sí. Allí trabaja, de ocho de la mañana a una de la tarde." Satisfied with my response the men thanked us and I, with ease, waved them good-bye.

"Do you know what you just did?" Reina asked as soon as the door clicked shut. "You just told them . . . told them . . . everything!"

Her green eyes bore into me, anger mixed with fear on her face. "I am telling your father as soon as he walks through the door!" She turned around and left me standing in a pool of confusion. What had I done? What was Reina talking about? I only said the name of the school where Mami worked and when she could be found teaching there.

With a jolt, I grasped what she meant by "them": Escuadrones de la Muerte. The death squads that had killed Señor Cabrera. I connected the dots Reina had perceived as soon as I had opened the door: Dubious men wanted to know where Mami worked . . . Why? Maybe so they could ambush her . . . and maybe even kill her! This was a very real possibility and I, in my eagerness to show Reina I could be a grown-up, had perhaps given my mother away. I liked to think that when my parents were not home I, not she, was in charge. ¡Dios mío! Reina was right! What had I done? I climbed the stairs up to my room and with each rung the horror of the situation unfolded before

July 9 – Overnight grave disturbances and bomb explosions reported in San Miguel. The ERP took responsibility.

July 10 – Napoleón Estrada, assistant principal of Instituto Thomas Jefferson, was killed in the city of Sonsonate.

---

me. I felt as if a hundred moths, harbingers of death, had flown into the house at once and shaken their bleak wing dust over everything, walls, furniture, my face.

"Do you know what you have done?" Papá asked when he stepped into my room.

"Sí," I said, barely looking up at him from my bed where I was sitting.

Actually, Reina didn't exactly tell me what I'd done wrong and Papá, I could tell, was not about to explain anything to me either, but I knew I'd not only corroborated where Mami lived and worked but laid out to perfect strangers her daily routine.

"Turn over," Papá commanded.

I did as told. I laid my belly on the bed and when my cheek touched the bed's flowery coverlet, I heard the swoosh of his belt as it travelled through his trousers' loops. The licks were swift and sharp on my buttocks and bare legs. The welts sprung up immediately.

"Me duele más que a vos," he said and then left the room.

He always said the same thing. I didn't believe it for a second. How could it hurt him more than me when my pain violently manifested itself on my skin?

I stayed put in the room and from my window watched night's fall. At some point, my bedroom door cracked open. Camila poked her head in but decided to leave me alone. Mami rushed into the bedroom as soon as she'd heard it all from Reina. She sat on the bed next to me and I melted into her. The adults made a round of phone calls. It was decided that Mami, my sister, Reina, and I were to pack an

---

July 10 – Bombs continue to explode throughout San Salvador.

July 12 – Thirty-one cadavers found in various locations in Santa Ana.

overnight bag and walk over to Tía Dalia's. Papá was staying behind in case "they" came back.

Once the decision was announced Papá went around the house collecting every incriminating document he could find, anything that disclosed his ties to the university and the teacher's union, any book that hinted at his political leanings. He put the documents and books into two cardboard boxes. Then he went into the third and least-used bedroom in the house, took down a few white panels from the false ceiling, and motioned for me to help him hoist the boxes up. After he was sure they would not collapse, he snapped each of the panels back into place.

As he did all this, I followed him around the house.

I wanted to hug him.
I wanted to tell him how sorry I was for what I had done.
I imagined him hugging me back and telling me that
he loved me, that no matter what happened he still loved me.

In the stale evening light, I thought I saw the grave iridescence of the moth's dust clinging to his fingertips. Our overnight stay at Tía Dalia's turned into a week. Our own residence was now marked, and we could no longer risk to inhabit it. Through connections my parents found another two-story house in nearby Colonia Sátelite and in a matter of days we settled in. The two boxes of books went from hovering above our heads in Colonia Miralvalle to resting under our feet in Colonia Satélite. In the new house the space under the stairs had

July 12 – About 100 people took over the Costa Rican embassy; among them are the elderly, women, and children from the organization LP-28. The policeman stationed at the entrance was killed.

July 12 – The former mayor of San Vicente, an ex-member of the right-wing organization ORDEN, a female employee, and a male security guard were killed.

---

been left untiled. Noticing this, ever the gardener, Papá exclaimed, "Unos helechos se verían bien bonitos aquí!," rattling off the names of the shade-tolerant houseplants he could grow there. A few days later, Papá shoveled a hole deep enough for the book boxes. He was no longer planting seeds. He was planting our survival. There was no apparent scar left on the ground after he finished interring the boxes. The soil would not give them, and by extension us, away.

Weeks later, while finishing breakfast and still in our nightgowns—peach, mine, and pink, Camila's—the *ratatata* of machine guns followed by the *piong, piong, piong* of revolvers started a macabre call-and-response that went on for hours. Explosions punctuated the exchange.

Reina told Camila and me to crouch underneath the stairs where Papá had hidden the two boxes with books. Our knees scraped the dirt floor. Reina, too tall to crawl underneath the stairs, sat facing us, her skirt tenting around her folded legs as she sat on the tile floor. The barrage of bullets crescendoed and waned, crescendoed and waned. Then the gaps between gunfire and silence got wider and wider.

Reina made the call when it was time to come out. She took one look at my sister's face, wet with tears and snot, and at mine, put an arm around my sister and, looking at me, said, "Vayan a vestirse." With the sound of bullets still ricocheting in our heads, we went upstairs to start the day over. When we came back downstairs Reina said that she had seen people in the neighborhood walking past our house, going in the direction where the shots had rang. She'd seen people she knew, other women who worked with families, like her. It would be safe, she said.

July 14 – The completely destroyed bodies of two *La Crónica* journalists, editor-in-chief Jaime Suárez Quemain and photographer César Najarro, were found in Lomas de San Francisco.

July 14 – The political party PDC suggested an alliance between governmental, institutional, and private productive sectors to carry out a "Crusade for Peace."

My sister and I each held one of Reina's hands when we stepped out. Up ahead, a few houses past ours, we saw a small group gathered on the opposite side of the street looking intently at the house in front of them. When we reached them, we too stared hard at the house facing us. All the houses resembled one another in this new subdivision. The house we lived in was identical to the house we were now staring at. Every surface of the façade was riddled with bullets. Some windows were completely blown out; in others, shards remained in place.

In one downstairs window, a curtain's ragged shreds trembled in the breeze. The walls beyond the windows were covered in soot.

The street-facing windows in this house corresponded to my sister's and my parents' bedrooms. My bedroom window was in the house's rear façade, facing the backyard and the tree canopies of the ravine that flowed behind all of the houses. We stood in front of the desecrated house for what seemed a long time. I asked Reina to take us back home and she decided to go around the block rather than straight back down the street. As we looped around the corner, an open jeep drove past, a soldier driving. Other soldiers walked the length of the street. Several lifeless bodies, rumpled like laundry, laid on the jeep's open bed and my small hand tightened around Reina's.

Rain, shine, or shootouts, Reina did everything possible to prepare us for school. We no longer attended Escuela España and our new uniforms consisted of white button-down tops and light-blue checkered skirts. Reina ironed both to perfection. She soaked our knee-high socks in bleach and polished our black shoes to rival obsidian. She served us almuerzo, the midday meal, only if we were ready:

July 15 – Francisco Mendoza Mazariego, an executive of LANICA, has been sequestered.

July 15 – A substantial bomb exploded outside of Albert Einstein University.

bathed, powered, combed, and wearing our impeccable uniforms. One afternoon, walking the two blocks to catch the bus, Ruta 26, that would take us to our school, we saw a man's body lying half on the sidewalk, half on the road, two, three meters away from the bus stop. He wore a white undershirt and dark trousers. His right arm, extended upward, was twisted in an unnatural position.

"No mires," I said to Camila, squeezing her hand as we crossed the street.

"No miremos," I corrected myself. Looking would haunt us. We did not want to be haunted.

Even when I told my sister not to look I could not resist. Everyone gathered at the bus stop pretended to look away from the corpse. I looked down at my shoes, already dusty from our short walk.

At ten years old, Camila was living in a war and going through a pink phase. If little ponies and rainbows had been a thing in El Salvador at the time, she would have availed herself. In Colonia Satélite we had our own rooms for the first time and Camila dreamt in hers in all shades of rose. She asked if she could take ballet classes like her friends did—there was a studio near the school we attended. Mami and Papá acquiesced and bought her the dancewear she needed in her preferred pink shade. Reina was put in charge of taking Camila to the dance lessons on the afternoons they were held. Most lesson days I preferred to stay home alone, but occasionally I made the trip with the two of them for fun.

On this particular day, after the lesson ended, we and several other girls, along with their respective adults, walked to the bus stop around

July 16 – Teacher René Antonio Rivera Pérez was killed in Colonia Santa Lucía.

July 20 – After searching the schools Instituto Nacional General Francisco Menéndez and Escuela Panamá, security forces found leftist-leaning printed material.

the corner from the studio to catch Ruta 26. Suddenly, machine-gun rounds alternating with the puny sound of revolvers by comparison broke the calm. The shots were loud and persistent and close by and everyone at the bus stop, teenage students from the liceo around the corner, street vendors, women, children, ran into any open storefronts, hid behind trees, and crouched beside parked cards, desperate to take cover. Reina took our hands and led us running back in the direction of the dance studio. Others from the class waiting at the stop did the same. We could see, rounding the corner, that Don Mario, the instructor, was standing at the door's threshold waving for his students and any person running by to take refuge inside. Each stride we took in his direction resounded in my ears, my heart a pounding drum. *Any moment now*, I told myself, *a bullet will shred my back.*

Don Mario slammed the door shut behind as soon as we scuttled in. Camila and her dance mates, who moments earlier had pirouetted and plied joyfully in their leotards and pink stockings, now huddled in terror with their respective adults along the walls of the studio, which was really the living room in Don Mario's house. A flowery curtain separated his workspace from his living quarters. So as not to draw attention to his house, Don Mario kept the electrical lights off. The only light in the room filtered in through a set of narrow windows high up on the wall facing the street, which created an intimate environment for the ballet classes, but now that it was dusk the lack of light gave the space an uncomfortable feel. We were all aware that only a wall of bricks separated us from the barrage of bullets outside.

July 23 – About 4,000 campesinos have fled Torola in San Fernando, Jocoaitique, and various other cantones from Morazàn Department.

July 29 – Dr. Jose Alejandro Castro and his son were found assassinated. They had been kidnapped the 16th of July in San Miguel.

Don Mario, still wearing his dark tights and sleeveless leotard, paced the length of the room, asking everyone to stay calm.

"¡Ay, Dios mío, calmense por favor!"

"¡Ay, bendito sea!"

"God have mercy," he said over and over, clasping his hands to his chest as he walked back and forth in dramatized distress. I followed his to-and-fro: his limbs, his dancer's posture never compromised, his toes pointing outward. Watching Don Mario helped me not succumb to tears like some of the other girls already had, muffling their cries in their nannies' skirts. I needed the distraction he unwittingly provided to quiet the questions reverberating in my head:

When was the shooting going to end?

How would we get home now that bus service was disrupted?

Would we ever make it out of this room alive?

The battle raged on, and the heat from our nervous bodies mingled with the remnants of the afternoon's heat hanging low in the crammed space. The fact that we could only rely on our sense of hearing to figure out what was happening outside made it so that my mind wandered the long and, by now, familiar road tilled by fear. I drew up scenes of agony and gore and imagined the destruction we would find upon leaving our safe place. To my relief, when Don Mario opened the door to let us out, there was only the evening stillness and the lingering smell of burnt rubber.

Soon after the incident, Atiquizaya returned to us when Glenda came to live with us. It had been months since we had last seen Abuela and Tía Valeria or Cornelia and our other relatives in Santa

---

August 1980
Aug. 7 – Four decapitated men were found in front of Majestic Movie Theater.

Aug. 9 – The organization FDR announced a labor stoppage for the 13th, 14th, and 15th days of the current month to demand an end to the genocide being carried out by the current government, the Junta Militar Demócrata Cristiana.

Ana. I could not remember the last time I saw Josué. Traveling anywhere on open highways was done at great personal risk. Bus routes to and from San Salvador were routinely stopped by armed forces, all passengers asked to step down and searched. Any shred of incriminating evidence—a book, a university ID—was grounds enough to be dragged away. People taken were sometimes never again seen.

We lost the ability to check in with family and friends. Conversations between acquaintances, our mechanism for making sense of the reality we were living, almost ceased altogether. We could tell that our lived experiences did not match the official story, but we could not fully articulate what the real story was. It is hard to tell, even with four decades of hindsight, whether this was happenstance or the result of a deliberate strategy employed by the Salvadoran military. We were cordoned off from one another; this made us more vulnerable and more isolated physically and psychologically.

Even within San Salvador, getting about town was risky. I'd lost hope to see or speak with Jorge ever again. In those days, Papá dared only to travel on his own, and less frequently, to visit our family in Atiquizaya. He did not want to risk traveling with Camila and I or all of us together as a family.

"¿Para que va a venir?" Mami asked when Papá told her that on his last visit he had been asked to keep Glenda in San Salvador for a few days.

"¡No podemos tenerla aquí!" Mami insisted.

"Ahora ya les dije que sí," was Papá's answer. It was done. He said yes when they asked him. He was not backing out on his word.

Aug. 9 – Four campesino families, 26 individuals in total, were killed in the rural area known as Dulce Nombre in Department of Chalatenango.

Aug. 11 – The Commerce and Industry Board, the Armed Forces, and members of ANEP make a call for people not to honor the work stoppage called by the FDR.

I knew Glenda was sick; I'd heard Papá say so. But standing before us, Glenda, who had always been thin, was now gaunt. Her fair skin was sallow, her beautiful almond-shaped eyes distant and receding inside their sockets. She seemed to shiver when the rest of us walked around complaining about the heat. She insisted again and again that she was being followed. They were coming, she knew it, she said. Glenda anticipated the knock on the door that would take her away, or the ambush on the street by one of the death squads. She sought refuge so far into herself that the shadow of her paranoia preceded her. But she appeared happy to see us again. She examined us from her precarious place, her new normal, and answered our questions with calmness but with none of the glow she once had.

It took some sleuthing on my part to figure out what Glenda had done that had made her descend into what seemed like madness. She had fallen in love with a young man in Atiquizaya who was involved with the guerrillas. She became involved. She leafleted neighborhoods, pasted notices on lampposts. As a dressmaker, she made shirts and facemasks for combatants. Then her love interest moved away, leaving her alone and afraid. At night her fears bourgeoned. She wandered in our house in her nightgown, sometimes knocking on my parents' bedroom door. I slept in the room adjacent to theirs and could hear her afflicted whispers, the urgency and worry in her voice:

"Don Roman, ahí vienen," she'd say. They are coming!

"No viene nadie." No one is coming, Papá would say in a calm tone.

"¡Vaya a acostarse!" Mami would say, insisting that Glenda go back to bed.

Aug. 12 – The Government Junta asks people to reject the work stoppage and go to work instead.

Aug. 12 – Transmission systems and gas distribution systems were dynamited, causing a blackout.

For Glenda, every gunshot, rumble, and night screech was a signal, evidence that "they" had found her. She did not stay long with us. Mami could not take it, maybe because her own nerves were stripped to raw cables. Whatever the reason, Glenda was sent away, back to Atiquizaya. The war crushed her gentle spirit. She was never able to regain her former self.

Meanwhile, our visa process continued. My parents culled and submitted financial records, work and salary histories, proof of savings. There were long forms to fill out, recommendation letters, bank statements, police records, property deeds, education records, birth certificates, photographs, interviews both in El Salvador and in the US. The paperwork had to be notarized and even translated. Mami stressed over visiting various government offices when it was dangerous to be out on the streets. She proceeded from one office to the next, waited in lines, all the while trying to keep a low profile to escape the eye of the ubiquitous informants. Our futures hinged on the embassy's acceptance of our application. The shootings remained constant. Sometimes near, sometimes far away.

Mami also stressed over the expense of filing the paperwork. I remember seeing her folded over the dining room table with frustration, shedding tears the day she found out that the US embassy had rejected a set of photographs due to the fact that her hair was obstructed. Ever stylish and on top of fashion trends, she had worn a colorful pañuelo on the day she went to have the photographs taken. The embassy demanded new photos. She thought their objection was idiotic. But she was also frustrated by the expense that taking new pictures required.

Aug. 15 – Ten dead in Cuidad Satélite, a neighborhood of San Salvador, after the work stoppage was declared a failure, setting off armed encounters across the city.

Aug. 16 – Francisco García Beltrán was killed in cold blood by extremists. He was pulled down from the bus he was riding on the road between San Salvador and Santa Ana.

Even biometric data had to be submitted. All four of us took and turned in lung x-rays, presumably to check for tuberculosis. My parents walked the "placas," x-ray films, which were very large, in a huge manila folder to the US embassy. Advice poured from friends and family about what to do, and what not to do. It so happened that I had an upcoming dentist visit and while cleaning my teeth the dentist identified a small cavity. She strongly suggested to Mami, who was in the room with me, that it would be wise, as a preventive measure, to have my molars—even cavity-free ones—drilled and filled. Mami had been counseled that it was best to complete any outstanding dental work in El Salvador, as this type of medical care was prohibitively expensive in the US. My mother, afraid of future insurmountable medical bills, agreed with the dentist. As a result, I received silver fillings in all of my molars.

On a regular day, Camila and I left for school before our parents arrived from their morning teaching jobs. Reina served us lunch before we left and an hour later my parents arrived from their respective schools to eat the midday meal. One early afternoon I came downstairs calling after Camila to hurry up or we'd miss the bus and was startled to find Papá sitting at the dining room table. He had come home from work early and was already in his white undershirt. Whenever he came into the house from the glare and heat of the midday sun, he'd take off his button-down shirt, slip out of his shoes and socks, and slide into his plastic house sandals.

"¡Buenas tardes, Papá!" I said, surprised to see him.

"Buenas," he said with a cheeky smile, noticing my shock.

Aug. 23 – Members of the electrical union demanded better wages and back pay and executed an energy blackout across the country that lasted 24 hours.

Aug. 25 – The government imposes a National Emergency.
Aug. 27 – Thirty people were killed in Soyapango in a fight with the army after 50 individuals detonated dynamite in a diesel plant.

"¿Qué está haciendo aquí tan temprano?" I was puzzled. How was he here so early?

"Salimos temprano hoy. Tu Mami viene al ratito" Ah. Teachers had an early release.

Mami would arrive soon, he'd said. Too bad Camila and I needed to be on our way, otherwise we could have all eaten the midday meal together. On our way out, Reina adjusted Camila's hair clip. The back door was more practical, offering a direct route from the dining room, through the kitchen and enclosed courtyard, to the street. When I opened the metal door, the hairs on the back of my neck stiffened. A full-sized military tank attempted to turn the corner meters away from our house. While its enormous caterpillar-encased wheels spun to make the right turn, its turret and main gun were aimed directly at our house. *¡Vienen por él! They are coming for Papá!* I yelled silently into the crater I had become.

I had recently learned through my careful eavesdropping that Papá was a wanted man. I overheard so much when adults gathered. Too many of his friends and colleagues had been killed. Here was the evidence that confirmed my intelligence gathering. Why else would there be a full-sized tank in our residential neighborhood?

I spun around and flung the metal door shut. It smacked the frame, creating a loud, reverberating bang. I realized that I had just drawn unwanted attention to our house. In two strides, I was back in the dining room standing across the table from Papá. He was still sitting where I'd left him, his back to the window with views of the backyard suffused in midday light.

Aug. 27 – Eleven buses were burned in Aytuxtepeque's bus terminal.
September 1980
Sept. 1 – Roberto Flores Velásquez, director of membership for ANDA, was assassinated in his car in Colonia Santa Lucía.

**Sept. 5 – Coronel Majano has stated that there is a military crisis.
Sept. 10 – Thirty-five campesinos were killed in the San Pedro Perulapán cantones El Rodeo, Tecoluca, La Esperanza, and San Francisco when the area was attacked by 300 insurgents.**

"¡Papá, hay un tanque allí afuera!" There is a tank outside! I said it quickly and with consternation in my voice. But what I really meant to say was, "They've come for you!"

He looked up from the newspaper, another of his habits before lunch, and in a calm voice said, "No te preocupes, váyanse a la escuela. Se les va ha hacer tarde." Don't worry. Go on to school. It will soon be late.

"Pero . . ." But . . . The lump in my throat did not allow me to make more words. Despair tangled up with half-formed thoughts spun crazily and I could not bring myself to say what I feared. I dared not contradict his soft command to go on to school. I could not bring myself to tell him that I thought that was the last time I would see him, that I expected the doors to give way to kicks of heavy-booted soldiers aiming their guns at him, that I wanted him to escape, jump the backyard fence, run, run away, it didn't matter where to, if it was in the direction of life.

"Váyanse ya o pierden el bus," he said. Go now, otherwise you will miss the bus. The gauzy material that covered the dining room windows was now aglow from the intense light behind it. I nodded and left back through the door I had slammed minutes before. Camila walked next to me in her own spotless uniform, her hand inside my sweaty one, the tank now already past our house, crawling the length of our street. There would be people at the bus stop going about their day, on their way to work, to a class at the university or, like us, on their way to school. Maybe they also saw the tank, maybe they also felt they had something to hide, maybe they would not speak about it to anyone like I didn't speak about it to my little sister.

**Sept. 10 – Engineer Jorge Alfredo Lemus Peñate was gunned down in his home.
Sept. 12 – Juan Francisco Calderón Celis, a teacher, was gunned down in Colonia Jardines de la Hacienda.
Sept. 16 – Three bazooka rockets were fired at the American embassy.**

16

Sueños

Oakland, California, 2004

Months after my first visit with Noreen, powerful dreams surfaced. The visual fields of these dream sequences were formidable, their texture and sounds crystal clear, their colors sharp and vibrant. The dreams were pointing my awareness in a particular direction. But were they pointing behind to the past or toward the future? I treated them like Rorschach tests, wanting to make immediate sense of their shapes and gestures, but I needed time, a lot more time, to understand them. I needed to hold them and I needed to stop running.

Dream Sequence

Mami and I are the only ones waiting for a bus. It is afternoon and across from us is a large concrete building, a factory, with a double gate to allow cars to go into a fenced parking lot. I feel a premonition: The factory will explode any minute. I turn to run away as fast as possible and drag Mami along. We run with all our strength. Quickly, I realize that we are too slow to evade the force of the blast. I scream at Mami to throw herself flat on the ground. I do the same. With our bodies pressed to the asphalt, we hear the blast's roar, followed by the feel of the fireball. When we finally dare to stand up, we can see through thick smoke that the bus stop, the factory, the gate, all that was in front of us minutes before, is gone, burned to the ground. We are covered in black soot—the powder of the destruction. Everything around us smolders. We stand among glass shards, burning wood, ripped metal, and the stench of burnt rubber.

Dream Sequence

Mami paces nervously in and out of rooms of what appears to be our house, insisting, half yelling, that we must pack our clothes. "We have to go! Now!" she urges. "Take only what's necessary. Hurry up! Hurry up!" she repeats again and again. I don't understand what is happening, the sudden need to flee. With rising frustration, I rummage through my chest of drawers. I have no idea what to pack. No one says where we are going. Will it be cold? Will it be hot? Will there be water? The only directive is to hurry. Panic is in the air and each breath rushes through my nostrils, filling me with the free-floating anxiety. I pack without knowing our destination, unaware of who is coming or why I am going in the first place. Confusion swirls, annoyance burns. There are several T-shirts I really like and know I cannot take them all. In the bottom of a drawer, I find two brand-new T-shirts stamped with scenes of bucolic open fields. I stare at the fields. I consider the shirts. I don't want to leave them behind, but there is no more room in my bag.

Dream Sequence

I am in an open field. The ground is pocked with small craterlike holes. Charred trees dot the landscape. War machinery—tanks, jeeps, small recognizance vehicles, convoy trucks—are scattered about the terrain, abandoned, yielding to rust. A black bull appears at the edge of the field. I hear and feel its hooves digging into the dry ground as it gallops. It appears determined to ram me. I bolt in the opposite direction. I run hard, and soon my lungs sting, my thorax aches from the effort to fill my lungs with as much air as I can. My legs turn heavy, like concrete. A truck appears. It is moving slowly, slower than the bull, and I flay my arms, shout for help, and it moves in my direction. As it nears, I see that in the truck's bed are scores of desperate-looking people. They are escaping the devastation. I scream for help, and they extend their arms toward me. The truck never stops rolling. "Get closer!" the people shout. "Get closer so that we may hoist you up," they say. I hurl myself in their direction, scanning their faces intensely, hoping to recognize someone familiar. Just as I am about to fling myself into their waiting arms, I spot Papá ailing near a charred tree. The bull is still on the chase. But Papá appears hurt, hunched over and unable to move. The arms of folks are still eager and outstretched, inviting me toward them. I let the truck drive away and run toward my papá.

Dream Sequence

I wake up in El Salvador, walking up a steep street; as I climb, indigo hills appear in the distance. I pass by a church, rich in ornamentation; arabesques and saints protrude from its starched white walls. I cross myself. It is what Abuela would have done. In front of me a blooming San Andrés tree spills its yellow unopened buds and trumpet flowers onto the sidewalk. I step on the dropped buds, making them pop. A childhood game. Small crotons with thick variegated leaves—cream, red, green, thrive—hug the front façades of colonial adobe houses painted a variety of ice cream colors. I walk past a house turned museum and realize I had walked alongside it before. Maybe in another life. I step inside its tall doors and discover a festival underway; people crowd hallways and sit on high-banked corridors.

This must be San Vicente, I tell myself. In my non-dream life, I've never been to that town on the eastern side of the country, but in the dream, I am certain that is where I am. I mingle in the main square, noticing people and things. Minutes turn to hours. I see people's brown faces, their short statures, cheeks and foreheads wrinkled by relentless sun, by back-splitting work, wrinkled from battling life. Yes. It was like that. People everywhere lost in conversation, assenting, agreeing.

An open door leads to an exhibition space. The exhibit consists of murals projected on whitewashed adobe walls. *This is the history of El Salvador!* I tell myself. The projected murals reach from floor to ceiling and depict scenes that one can read as belonging to different epochs relevant to the country: before human habitation, pre-Columbian times, colonial times to the present. But the events are not shown in any kind of historical sequence. I try to order the scenes chronologically without success as the murals rotate and their images and colors, faces, landscapes, merge with one another.

I stay for a while suspended in the magic of the telling. *It doesn't matter when what was,* they seem to tell me, *what matters is that you are here today, right now, and you are part of this history cascading down these walls. A history that is not linear but something that returns and curls in on itself.* When I decide to leave I find no exit. All doors have disappeared. I panic and dash from one corner of the space to the other, calling out for help, feeling the walls for a trapdoor or a secret exit, the colors and images of the murals projecting all over my body. Every time I think I've found the door through which I entered, a mural projects onto the wall, crashes over it, dissolves it with its flashing images.

Eventually, miraculously, I am let out into the middle of a craft fair. Sculptures made from petrified black lava, painted in intense colors, giant vases with architectural details, mangoes, guavas, all sorts of fruit rendered in clay and painted in shades of rainbow are for sale. Everything is colorful and splendid. My eye devours textiles on display, each embroidered with luminous threads and executed in exquisite detail. I can't drink in their dazzling beauty fast enough. I wonder how to fit these treasures into the suitcase I'm suddenly carrying. Then I remember I already bought presents for family and friends. I am in this space, breathing this air, and the sidewalks, the people, the trees, the richness of it all, is a haven of warmth and color. I am familiar with all of it, all of it is inside me.

17

We Belonged to Each Other

San Salvador, El Salvador, 1980

After breakfast I settled down with a book in the shady nook in our backyard where our house met our neighbor's. My back rubbed against the cinder block wall while my bare feet rested on the cool grass. Reina and Camila were both inside the house. A sudden whip of helicopter blades tore through the morning's tenderness. The uproar turned tree canopies into disheveled manes and the rotor wash subjugated the patio's grass, which struggled to stay tethered to the ground. I looked up just in time to see the tip of a rotating blade emerging above the roofline of our house, then the helicopter's nose became visible. I drew my legs up to my chest as if willing a defensive shell. My breathing raced. A sick sensation built up in my stomach

---

Sept. 18 – The group FDR took over the OEA (Organization of American States) headquarters. The group demanded freedom for political prisoners, a stop to the political repression, the lifting of the state of emergency, and the expulsion of armed forces from the national university.

Sept. 18 – Seven bombs exploded in various parts of San Salvador.
Sept. 22 – The body of Esperanza Quijano, who was 24 years old, was found in Santa Ana.

---

and an inner voice, clear and commanding, spoke to me: *No te muevas. Don't move.*

The helicopter hovered above our house, facing the direction in which we had heard balazos earlier in the morning. Its right door slid open. A man dressed in fatigues leaned forward, resting his right leg on the landing skid. *No te muevas,* the inner voice commanded once again. *Don't flinch!* I told myself. Sunglasses and a large helmet hid the soldier's face. He rested a machine gun on his thigh. Over the crunch of the helicopter blades, I could hear gunshots somewhere nearby.

No te muevas, the voice spoke again. Frozen in place, unable to take my eyes off the soldier's black lace-up boots, I fought with the visceral terror of imagining his machine gun aimed at me. Then, as suddenly as it had appeared, the helicopter slipped away from my line of sight. The terror released me. I felt limp. That is when I noticed her: Reina standing in the door's threshold staring at me. How long had she been there?

"¿Qué esta haciendo niña?!" she asked, throwing her arms up in the air. What do you think you're doing?! I knew she wanted to scream at me. She wanted to say: *You almost got killed!* I wanted to explain, but there was no wind in my body to make words.

Yet, even if I could have explained anything, I wouldn't have known what I'd be explaining. I didn't know what I had been doing with my back against the cinder block wall, knees to my chin, my arms hugging my legs.

Reina continued to stare and I knew that she knew that I could have been a target if the soldiers in the helicopter had seen me, and

---

October 1980
Oct. 2 – Seven men were killed in a billiards bar in Ayutuxtepeque. They were lined up against a wall and executed.

Oct. 6 – A bomb exploded at the entrance of the Archbishop's headquarters.

she could have been killed if she had stepped into the patio to drag me inside the house. We each had controlled our natural instincts to move. We stayed affixed to our spots and that had saved us. Afterward, the day went on as usual. Reina served us almuerzo and we ate in our white button-down shirts and sharply ironed checkered skirts. So many shocks each day. Stones gather moss; birds cull reeds, twigs, to build their nests. We gathered shocks, horrors, fears, and shared them with no one, letting them drift and roam in the tunnels of our unconscious.

Soon after, Papá came home with unbearable news. Lauro and the resistance group he was traveling with were ambushed by police in Santa Ana. The group was walking on a busy street when the police opened fire upon recognizing them. A street fight ensued, forcing Lauro and the group to take refuge inside a convent from which they took a defensive position. After several hours the police entered the convent, killing everyone in the group.

From our house in San Salvador, I imagined how my family in Atiquizaya was reacting to the news. Lauro's sisters Cornelia and Magdalena, his parents, his brothers, all of them, in the open corridor of their house folding into one another. The fire was surely burning and on el poyo, a pot of beans must have been simmering and against the embers, a pot of black coffee. The oxen a stone's throw away must have chewed morros rhythmically as they always did, their eyes affixed to the arc of our collective grief. There was no telephone in their house for us to call, no way to run across the street over the cobblestones into their adobe house to offer condolences. No way to

Oct. 7 – About 14 campesinos were killed in El Sitio, Department of Ilobasco. Local authorities blamed leftist insurgents for the act.

Oct. 7 – The body of Maria Magdalena Hernández, secretary of the National Human Rights Commission, who was kidnapped a week ago, was found today on the road to La Libertad.

wrap one another in our arms, to grieve together. There was no regal mango tree to climb in our San Salvador backyard, no flowers to behead, no rose bushes from which to tear perfumed petals and crush between our fingers as a way of finding solace.

Years later, on a visit to El Salvador, Tía Valeria and Magdalena, Lauro's older sister, shared with me what they remember of Lauro's death. They told me that Doña Merced heard the names of the dead in the convent's ambush while making tortillas for the noon meal. With her hands wet and clumped with masa from making the noon tortillas, she ran this way and that screaming, "¡Mi hijo, mi hijo!" Carlos, one of Lauro's older brothers, and Tía Valeria traveled to the morgue in Santa Ana to identify the body. Tía Valeria said that despite the bullets in his body and the one that tore through his head, it was unmistakably Lauro. She remembered that one of the policías in the room where the dead had been laid stepped forward and boasted that it was he who had shot the bullet that shattered Lauro's face. Magdalena shared that he was six days away from his twenty-third birthday.

In the adobe house where I played as a child, a house Lauro knew well, my cousin Magdalena's grief for her fallen younger brother filled the volume of Tía Valeria's living room. It was as if the words my tía and my cousin spoke conjured Lauro's body forty-two years after his assassination and the three of us could finally grieve together. I didn't have to see them to know that high in the rafters, the scorpions felt the weight of our sorrow and, for a while, held their tails in check. When Lauro was murdered, we lived in a country where we

Oct. 8 – A woman and her four children were assassinated in Finca Las Luces, Department of Santa Ana. One of her children, a young woman who was pregnant, was found decapitated.

Oct. 9 – In the Department of Usulután, José Napoleón Duarte, member of the Government Junta, stated that the government is not killing people or detonating bombs, and that those actions are the work of leftist extremists.

were marked for death simply by association. To protect ourselves, we needed to keep quiet about his death.

After Lauro's killing, things took on dimensions I did not think were possible and even ordinary events like going to the market for the weekly shopping became extraordinary. Running errands with Mami one day, we passed by a church, and in a move completely out of the ordinary, she strolled inside. Votives flickered in the semi-darkness. Mami guided me to a pew and there she kneeled and bowed her head in prayer. Moments of devotion like this belonged to my abuela. To kneel and pray with one of my parents had always resided in the province of my desires. It was ironic that "la situación," as we called the unofficial war we lived in, made my dear wish come true. Under the thick veneer of Mami's modernity lived a woman like my abuela, who was not afraid to show her vulnerability and dared ask God and neighbors for help if she needed it. We left the church and stepped into the bright day and all I could think of was that we must be in great danger for Mami to pray with such devotion.

As far back as 1974 embassies had been targets of aggression and hostile takeovers by the guerrillas. The Chilean, Argentine, and Guatemalan embassies were bombed. In 1979 the French and Costa Rican embassies were taken over. It was known that the US provided financial support, military weapons, training, and intelligence to the Salvadoran government. As a result, the US embassy was fortified to prevent attacks. A thick wall was constructed around its perimeter. A big security gate controlled who went in and out of the building. Armed guards stood ever alert at its entrance and around its

Oct. 9 – The body of the priest Manuel Antonio Reyes Mónico has been found in San Luis Mariona, Cuscatancingo.

Oct. 9 – A spokesman from the Armed Forces reported that in "La Reubicación San Bartolo" Depto. Chalatenango, insurgents shot dead a family.

boundary. These defensive measures gave the embassy a foreboding feeling. As the process with the travel permits advanced, my parents visited the US embassy several times to drop off required documents. The culminating appointment was an in-person interview with the then-United States ambassador to El Salvador, Robert E. White.

I accompanied Mami on one of her visits to the embassy. To get there, we took several buses that wove through downtown San Salvador until the last bus dropped us off at the bottom of a hill. The embassy sat at the very top. As we hiked up I spotted a woman and a girl who appeared to have just left the embassy. They stood on the same side of the street as us, while the armed sentinels flanking the entrance gate looked on. The girl, who seemed closer to Camila's age, held the woman's hand loosely. Both had blondish hair that fell to their shoulders and I assumed they were an American mother-daughter pair. I observed the slackness and ease of their bodies, recognizing something between them that Mami and I did not have, but which my heart wanted for us: a sense of lightness, a freedom, the certainty of a new day.

When I was little, I liked to sneak into my parents' room for no particular reason, maybe to imagine myself as a grown-up. A grown-up like them: bright, agile, capable, hard working. I perused whatever papers, magazines, or books lingered on their bedside tables. I examined Papá's pencils, which he sharpened with neat and efficient strokes using a loose blade. I tried out the blade on one of my own pencils, launching into a low stroke. Instead of lifting a chip of wood away from the graphite, the blade sunk into my right index finger.

Oct. 10 – The South African ambassador Archibald Gardner Dunn, who was sequestered by the organization FPL in November 1979, was executed according to a communiqué from said organization.

Oct. 16 – Coronel Jaime Abdul Gutierrez of the Government Junta pleaded with young people who have been involved in violent activities and who have joined left wing groups to return to the heart of their families and offered them amnesty.

Blood squirted, some of it landing on the bed's coverlet. I ran out of the room seeking help from our muchacha. Alarmed, she asked, "¿Qué pasa?" when she saw my bloodstained hand. I fainted.

In 1980, walking into my parents' private space had more to do with finding refuge, with seeking solace and security among their belongings, than with curiosity. Several times while visiting their bedroom I watched army jeeps doing reconnaissance in our neighborhood. But as the war that was not yet a war marched on, the jeeps had turned into small, armored vehicles, or tanquetas, as we called them. Even full-blown tanks came to patrol our streets. The tanks were completely out of scale in our residential neighborhood of narrow streets and windowed curtains. This was a place of muchachas on errands, children walking to school, and folks on their way to work. It was a sight to behold, a behemoth tank spinning an awkward turn on its caterpillar treads at the corner of our narrow street.

By the time fully armored tanks started showing up in our neighborhood, all of our paperwork to emigrate to the US had been submitted, lawyers consulted and paid, photographs issued, and interviews at the US embassy in San Salvador completed. In early November our paperwork was approved. Our departure was imminent. There was no family gathering, no Sunday supper to celebrate. Leaving was necessary but not welcomed. The visa news brought relief, but I could not say it brought joy.

In a move that defied all the warnings the adults had given us, I climbed over the cinder block fence at the back of our house to explore a section of the ravine that flowed behind it. It was not the

Oct. 20 – Eleven dead found on the main road to Sonsonate. Three found in Ilopango. Seven persons found dead in Texistepeque. Four persons found in Ciudad Delgado.

Oct. 24 – Dr. José Mauricio Velásquez was shot in his clinic. No one took responsibility.

---

first time I had jumped the fence. When I'd done it, Camila and our three cousins, Tía Dalia's youngest children, had joined me. We could see the lush canopies of mango and almendra de río trees that clustered along the ravine from the top of the fence. The five of us found a way to climb the fence and land safely on the other side, then scampered down the dirt path to the edge of the ravine. Once there, we delighted in knocking down ripe mangoes with stones. Sometimes we slung obscenities at the blue sky for no particular reason. We returned home sweaty and muddy and happy. Adventures down to the ravine became our coveted secret.

I'd noticed that on the ravine's opposite bank a lane picked up past the thicket of reeds and trees. As the oldest and the most capable to navigate the steep path, I decided to investigate on my own. I don't know what compelled me. There were moments when the world closed in on me in a good way, when being alone didn't mean being afraid. Like sitting in our previous backyard sketching insects and leaves. Or lying on the grass of Tía Dalia's tidy backyard looking up at the stars. At those moments, in my aloneness, I could feel and relish the intimacy of things.

The dirt path on the ravine's far side was narrow and ran close to the water. It eventually opened up, leading to a tugurio, a slum, tucked among the riverbanks. Mud houses shored up with cardboard and tin sheets lined the dirt road. I pretended to know where I was going but was startled by the rachitic houses and equally rachitic young children milling about. From a ways away, I saw a group of people spilling out of one of the huts. Up close I understood a wake

---

Oct. 24 – Doctor Pedro Novoa Flores, former secretary of the Supreme Court, was assassinated.

Oct. 25 – Two bombs exploded in the Jesuit residence of the University of Central America.

was underway. I walked up to the hut and joined the line to go inside. I knew no one, yet no one shooed me away. Inside was cramped and very dark. The only light emanated from a few candles set around the coffin laid on a bare table. This was death's chamber—nothing else fit inside it.

A small open lid revealed a man's face. Even in death his youth shone through. His eyes were closed, and his black hair combed neatly to the side, his cheeks peppered with tiny acne craters. His corpse held a lemon in his mouth. The fruit's tart sunshine contrasted with his ashen skin and with the lugubrious pallor of the room. Bent over the small window I crossed myself like everyone before me had done and turned back to the light outside. Nothing in the room, not the dead body, nor the people to whom he belonged, nor the neighbors or relatives or whoever they were, made me feel afraid.

My senses, highly trained to fear, were not triggered even though I was in a completely unfamiliar environment. Sounds were suspended somehow inside and around the hut. There was no bark from the ubiquitous stray dog, no trace of birdsong cascading from the nearby trees, no whispers from the women huddled in pairs at the entrance of the hut, no wisps of sobs from those glued to the walls inside the room, no muffled prayers from a grandma who was surely there, just a silent stream of visitors going in and out of the hut.

Things could have happened. But among those people I felt safe. I was one of them, and they let me be among them. Our very near future could be that of the man on the table; we all knew it and that thought humbled and united us. Bullets made us hyper alert.

Oct. 29 – University of El Salvador professor Félix Antonio Ulloa and the person who accompanied him, Francisco Alfredo Cuéllar, were killed.

November 1980

Nov. 2 – Ten cadavers belonging to unidentified young men were found on the road to Apulo.

Death gave us silence. A reprieve. The face of the man framed by the small casket door, the yellow of the lemon, the silence, swirled in me. Why a lemon? Was it to prevent a possible stench from the corpse? Was his ghost watching us from a nearby tree? I crossed the brook and scampered up the hill in a trance, mechanically pushing and clearing the way through the soft thicket growing and spilling onto the path. I wanted to ask Reina about the use of the lemon, but asking would reveal my transgression. I jumped the fence back into the familiar order: Reina cleaning and cooking, books on shelves, homework to do.

I was a month away from turning fourteen when my parents asked me to join them in their bedroom. When I came in, they were standing next to their bed. Mami pulled a white envelope from the drawer of her bedside table. She held it up for me to see it while my father spoke: "In case something happens to us," he said. There were no theatrics when he said this; his voice was calm and steady.

I stood facing them; the sun setting behind them slowly turned them into speaking shadows. Their action confirmed what I had feared for months, perhaps years. My parents were as susceptible as other teachers, workers, priests, friends, family members, acquaintances who had been disappeared or murdered. I held on to the only thing I had: silence. Dread flushed through me the instant my father spoke. And questions. So many of them.

Did the envelope have money?

Which of Mami's sisters or Papá's sisters was willing to take us in?

Would Camila and I stay together?

Nov. 4 – In an ambush led by insurgents from the organization FPL, Manuel de Jesús Rivas Rodriguez, general manager of the International Fair, was killed.

Nov. 7 – A thirteen-year-old boy and four adults were killed in Santa Ana.

Would we be split up?
Could Camila and I be able to still go north, by ourselves?
Would Tía Maura, who lived in West Palm Beach, want us?
Who would want us?

Asking meant accepting the reality they were presenting. And I needed to be brave, for them and for myself. I feared for my parents' lives, and I feared for my own. I lived expecting to be caught in a street battle or to catch a stray bullet in the street or in our own living room. But my biggest fear became that Papá would one day not come home. Like someone carrying a religious medallion around their neck to protect them, I carried the fear of Papá's death around my neck, and instead of infusing hope and valor my badge debilitated me—a perverse tropical kryptonite. The weight of the chain became part of my weight. It appeared on the scale clearly, but only I could read it; as such it would have escaped years of wellness visits to the doctor. Somehow Mami, who as a teacher was just as vulnerable, was never part of my nightmares. My imagination would not take me there. She was untouchable. In my recurring worst-case scenarios, I needed her to survive. Always. I imagined my death, my father's death, but in my nightmares Mami and Camila always remained alive.

"It is in this drawer," Mami said, placing the envelope there

I nodded and waited for more, but no one said anything else. We looked at one another like statues in an unnamed plaza who endure snow, bitter wind, cold rain, spring sunshine, the lushness of summer air, trapped as they are in their bronze castings. There was absolutely no gallantry there, no pat on the shoulder. No hug. Facing the

---

Nov. 13 – The political organization DRU and the FPL, ERP, PCS, and RN have affirmed their operating under one leadership: one political and military strategy.

Nov. 16 – Coronel Carlos Alfredo Choto, his wife, and their two children died inside their burning house the result of bombs.
Nov. 17 – Ten cadavers found near Apopa.

---

moment is what had to be done. I nodded. I acknowledged that I understood what was at stake and what to do in case it came to pass. Look for the envelope on the right-hand side of Mami's bed and never say anything to anyone. Better to keep the fear under lock and key than to make it active by sharing it with others, letting it flourish and thrive in all the ways that it would surely want to go.

*

I wish the way my parents told me about the envelope would have been different. I wish it had gone like this: The summoned daughter, upon hearing her father speak, crumbles and sits on the bed sobbing as her mother comes to embrace her. Or she races to embrace her mother or father or both, and her parents reassure her. Hug her. Tell her that this is only some remote precaution. Nothing will happen to them. All will be well. In another one of my dreamt-up versions, the parents invite the girl to sit between them on the bed where they gently explain the situation, tell her how scared they are themselves, hold her, tell her how much they love her and her sister. I play with different versions of the story. I try them on like dresses over the memory of what happened.

Maybe my parents were already defeated by the incessant violence we endured, defeated by burying friends when it was dangerous to pledge allegiance to a loved one in public, and haunted by the guilt that festered for having survived their friends or for having skipped a funeral when it became clear that paying last respects by standing

---

Nov. 26 – Forty-seven left dead in a fight in Soyapango, reported the Armed Forces after it attacked a guerilla camp in Plan de Pito, Soyapango.

Nov. 27 – Seven leftist leaders were abducted from the Socorro Juridico del Arzobispado in San Salvador and later found assassinated.
Nov. 29 – Five cadavers were found in Sonsonate's cemetery. Death squads took responsibility.

---

alongside a friend's coffin was condoning your own death sentence. In retrospect, I see that the rigidity we clung to is what kept us upright. A word is all that would have been needed for us to collapse under our own weight. Silence offered a screen, a kind mantle behind which to hide our fears. Perhaps they, like me, were numbed by the terror inherent in the possibility they presented. Maybe they were trying to be as brave as I was, and staying away from words insured their composure.

We could not travel to the eastern part of the country. We could not travel to the west. We could not travel to neighborhoods inside the city. We could not travel at night. We could not visit neighbors. We could not listen to or read anything that challenged the government. We could not attend funerals. Going to mass might be suspect. We monitored our conversations. After a while it was better not to make conversation at all. Soon the only border left was the skin of our bodies. We made silence and our silence grew inside us like weeds, prolific and unwanted, until it became the weather of our days.

One afternoon, with our departure days away, while traveling with Tìa Dalia in her red Datsun, she said, "Claudita, ahora que se van quiero decirte algo muy importante." Her voice was steady, her tone more serious than running errands deserved. A red flag went up inside me. She said she wanted to tell me something important.

"Si Tía," I said, making myself sound matter of fact.

"Cuando estén allá, quiero que cada mañana cuando te levantes y te veas en el espejo te digas, '¡Qué linda soy!' "

Nov. 30 – Various street vendor posts with thatched roofs caught fire after bombs detonated in the market of Ciudad Delgado.

December 1980
Dec. 1 – Eight members of the same family were killed in Metapán; six buses of Route 4 and seven other buses belonging to routes in San Salvador were burned.
Dec. 4 – Twelve dead were found today in the streets of San Salvador.

She was at the wheel and I in the rear seat; I could see her velvet eyes looking at me and feel the intensity of her wish for me. It sounded silly to do what she was suggesting: in our new life in the US, to tell myself I was beautiful every day I faced the mirror in the morning. I didn't feel beautiful in the morning—quite the opposite. She was deliberate. I was puzzled but accepted her offering and tucked it somewhere between my ribs and my heart.

Dec. 5 – Three American Maryknoll nuns—Ita Ford, Maura Clark, and Dorothy Kagel—and the lay missionary Jean Donovan were found dead in Santa Teresa. They were traveling to San Salvador from the International Airport.

Dec. 8 – From Rome, during the traditional ceremony to celebrate the Immaculate Conception, the Pope condemned "the murder of religious individuals in El Salvador" as "fratricide that has the country covered in bloodshed."

And you realize at that point that the Salvadoran military were out of control. I mean they would kill anybody.

—Robert E. White, US Ambassador to El Salvador (1980–81), Huntley Archives, 1980

Dec. 12 – The government of President Carter threatens to stop aid to El Salvador until the current government is restructured, including establishing a new High Military Command.
Dec. 17 – The United States government restarted its economic aid package of $20 million.

18

After the Long Night

Oakland, California, 2004

The implications of Noreen's PTSD diagnosis crushed me. If my life was impacted by PTSD, so was my sister's life and my mother's and my father's. Moreover, my cousins, aunts, and uncles, who'd lived through the entire twelve years of civil war in El Salvador, must suffer from it too. With a deafening roar, the biggest implication manifested before me: The entire country—soldiers, guerrillas, women, men, children, all Salvadorans, those who live in the country and those of us who left during those war years—must contend in one way or another with PTSD.

> What did it mean to accept the label?
> She suffers from PTSD.
> I suffer from PTSD.
> We suffer from PTSD.

To agree meant I was sick. I had not been well for a long time. How far back in the story of my family did I need to go to find the onset of this violence that corrodes me? Like a long line of stacked-up dominos, my PTSD was a chain reaction. To point a finger in any single particular direction was futile. The civil war, the terror and brutality of it, were only the tip of a very large iceberg: colonial brutality, machismo, poverty, the US imperialist agenda in Central America, all fed the mouth that devoured El Salvador.

Immediately after Noreen first introduced the term "PTSD" in our session, I felt a sadness that consumed everything in its path like fire consumes—without hesitancy. I wished to lie down and sleep for a long, long time. Nowhere in particular. On a grassy lawn looking at the night sky, in the rooms of the house in Atiquizaya, under a tamarind tree, among the muddy banks of a deep river. That day after my session, I wept all the way home. Edith, who looked after my babies, noticed my state but kept quiet. When John came home, I collapsed into bed. The next day I woke up still wearing my clothes from the day before.

The list of behaviors Noreen had read put a lot of my family's traits in context: My mother's inability after arriving in the US to hear anything positive or negative about El Salvador, her wish on some level to have nothing to do with it. My papá's recurrent nightmares of persecution when we first arrived. My own apocalyptic dreams. I began to understand the silence that padded our interactions, that stuck always to us. All these years of suffering, unable to name what we felt. So many years spent lost in a labyrinth of forgetting.

When we arrived in Florida, Papá washed dishes at a seafood restaurant on West Palm Beach's Military Trail and Mami tested circuit boards in an electronics factory. Hungry for up-to-date information, Papá figured out a way to fish for news about El Salvador on TV and on radio outlets transmitting in Spanish. Whenever a story about El Salvador made it into the *Miami Herald*, he labored to understand it, reading with a Spanish–English dictionary by his side. Sometimes he enlisted the help of my aunt, who is a fluent English speaker. What news he'd learn, he'd share with the rest of us over meals. Mami wanted none of it. She would listen to Papá's reports and comment, more often than not, with biting sarcasm. She never sought information herself; she had had enough. Her gaze was focused elsewhere, forward maybe, focused on forgetting perhaps. Wherever she was looking, it certainly was not at what we had left behind.

In another session with Noreen, I told her that some things dissolved me into sadness. It came over me suddenly and it stretched out endlessly in front of me. I could never see where it ended.

"Can you tell me what sort of things make you sad?" she asked.

"Everything," I said. "A sunset, a television commercial, even children's stories, stories of kids who've lost their parents, stories of girls in parts of the world who cannot go to school, survival stories," I said. She nodded.

"Say more."

"Sometimes when I am reading to my kids the feeling of sadness is so overwhelming it shuts me down, puts my voice out, like a spent candlewick. I am ashamed then, because in those moments I have no control over my emotions," I said.

"Why don't you bring one of those books to read here next time," she suggested. "Bring one of the books in Spanish."

El Señor Oso y el Oso made the trip up the hill with me the following week. Set in Spain, it is a tale about a rich but cantankerous old man who lives atop a hill in a giant empty house. The town's children have made him the butt of cruel jokes for being so serious. The man sees a chained and abused bear being exploited by a traveling jester. The man makes the bear "dance" by prodding its hind legs with a pointy steel rod. The bear skips and jumps in a rhythmic fashion as if really dancing, delighting the crowd. Angry with the abuse he witnesses, the old man decides to buy the bear. He pays handsomely for it, takes it to his estate, and breaks its shackles. Roaming the estate, the bear finds shelter under a grove of trees and falls asleep listening to the nearby brook. When he wakes up, next to him on the plush meadow grass, a pile of apples awaits him courtesy of the old man. It is a story of kindness, of respect for living things. It has a happy ending. Everyone wins: The man has a companion, the bear freedom, and the jester, money.

Settled on the leather sofa, I began to read out loud. When I got to the page where the old man buys the bear and takes him home, the lump that always formed in my throat as I read the book to Aurora surfaced, and from then on, I could read only intermittently. I could not have gotten through the rest of the book without the box of Kleenex tactfully placed on the side table.

The arrival of the bear to the old man's estate is a moment of triumph in the book. The bear has been rescued. It will no longer live chained, it will no longer be ridiculed and prodded with a pointed iron rod. The reader can foresee the bear's future freedom and the old man's satisfaction in providing it. But instead of providing me with the expected joy, the triumphant passage did the opposite. I was the bear who had endured abuse, hunger, pain, isolation, loss, then rescue. Freedom from misfortune implies the ability to feel like oneself once more. But what if one has never allowed oneself to fully feel her emotions? What if one has never let herself simply be because fear has clouded every judgment, every encounter? What do you do then? For me, the challenge and fear of owning my feelings negated the author's intended catharsis.

Having held on to fear all my life, even reading a scenario where duress is overcome proved too difficult. I could not have been further from danger in my toddler's softly lit room, sitting on her bed, surrounded with toys and books for her delight. I was not in harm's way in my therapist's office, sitting on the brown couch. But my body tensed, living the pain and abandonment of the bear. I had battled fear and sadness so long that I had come to inhabit fear and sadness. My trauma spoiled even the loveliest of moments: reading a bedtime story to my sweet toddler.

Now that I had become a parent myself I understood the weight upon my own parents' shoulders, the desperation they must have felt to protect us from the escalating violence. Camila and I were not toddlers, but we were their babies all the same. My parents were well into their forties when we escaped, seasoned teachers, Mami having recently completed an advanced degree at the university and Papá close to it. He was unable to finish his degree because the credit requirements were longer than those needed for Mami's degree and the university closed permanently due to the violence, leaving him unable to complete the necessary classes to graduate.

I remember Mami hosting study groups at our house; most of her fellow students were teachers with families, men and women who staked their sacrifice on behalf of their children's futures. On the days Mami hosted her classmates, our dining room table transformed into a cafeteria-style study hall, with ashtrays within hand's reach for everyone, hot coffee, and simple snacks. These teachers worked hard, comparing notes and clarifying concepts to one another. Now and then, someone would break the earnestness of the moment with a joke or a pun, and the table shattered with free-for-all laughter. Ever the observant girl, I watched them. I enjoyed the ease of their bodies, how they leaned into one another to hear better, a hand bringing a cigarette to the lips, an eager nod in approval.

Papá did not bring classmates home. His study sessions unfolded out in nature, where the trees he researched thrived. He shared his findings with us when he returned from his expeditions, talking about the growth habits and territorial density of particular species, their branching patterns and leafing tendencies. These experiences, the ability to speak freely, to gather at home with friends and colleagues, eventually dried up as a river dries up. People telling one another stories of their everyday—the very fabric of community—dried up as the reach of the government's repression widened and deepened. My parents' personhoods, the way they were in the world—he, earnest and diligent; she, curious and joyous—flattened, became unidimensional: he, worried; she, anxious.

By the time my parents made the monumental decision to leave the country they had already lost so much. They bet all they had on a tendril of hope that their choice to leave would yield a better life for their daughters. They advanced despite the fear they surely must have felt toward a place they had never seen, toward a language they had never spoken, propelled by valor and the indomitable wish to survive ablaze in their hearts.

19

A House to Call Home

Los Angeles, California, 1997

One of my first assignments as an urban planner graduate student was to write about the meaning of home. The professor argued that as professionals who were to design future communities, write housing policy, work with developers, or advocate for more affordable housing, we needed clarity with the concept. As she explained the assignment, I broke into an anxiety attack, my palms started sweating profusely, and focusing on the lecture became impossible. I felt the crest of a migraine and fled the classroom as soon as the lecture was over, terrorized by the idea of having to contend with my concept of home. No one had asked me that of me before. I could not see a way into or around the task. I let days go by without writing a word, procrastinating until the eve before the assignment was due, and then I wrote what I thought was expected.

To write about home, I first needed to write about the loss of home—my home. Without that step I could not attempt to articulate what home meant to me. The first wave of feeling that hit me upon hearing the assignment was of shame. After we left El Salvador, my parents could not afford to rent a house on their own. When we did inhabit a house it was because we moved in with other relatives and helped them with rent and other expenses. On their own my parents rented a series of apartments, some of them with worn-out brown carpets and with kitchens and bathrooms laid with linoleum floors that lifted at the corners. My parents made ends meet and put food on the table at great cost to their minds and bodies. Yet, they created home routines that supported Camila and I with our schooling. Rain or shine, tired or not, Mami cooked an evening meal and the four of us sat down to eat as we had done in El Salvador. I believe this routine alone helped me face many adversities at school. Like my father's gardening back in El Salvador, Mami's cooking in the US grounded me. When I was a senior in high school I needed to be at school at 6:30 A.M. for my driver's ed class; Papá walked me to school so that I would be safe, then walked back home before heading to work. I was learning to drive but my family did not yet have a car.

We survived together as a family, but we were also alone. Never in those apartments did we experience the communion with family and friends we had shared in our Salvadoran homes. We were keenly aware of that fact. Certainly before 1980, but even during that most terrible year, my parents hosted Tía Dalia and Tío Javier and Mónica for long lunches that broke into baseball games in the backyard where every single person present played, even toddler cousins. Afternoon coffee followed and with it, the inevitable adult conversation in hushed tones, while we children roamed the house making mischief.

We spent our first US winter in an apartment on the outskirts of Lodi, New Jersey. It was part of a large complex of low-income housing. The apartment became unbearably cold as winter progressed; a freezing draft blew through the rooms and ice clamped both the inside and outside of the single-pane windows. We were ill-prepared for the weather and had little means of availing ourselves of appropriate clothing. We did not have a car and so I walked the two miles to the high school in my thin-soled sneakers no matter what the day offered: rain, snow, slush. Twice a day I passed by an old, abandoned house; an overgrown thicket spilled from its front yard, trash defaced the perimeter of the property, and rats had surely made home of it. If only we could own it. I longed to make this house our own and imagined the many ways we would clean it; the many ways we would love it.

That day in my urban planning class I felt shame and was embarrassed at my family's lack of wealth and financial security when, in fact, I was only being poked by the iceberg of my loss. We lost our home when we left El Salvador, all the concentric iterations of it, from language, to country, to community, to family, to the structure of our house. My conversation with Cornelia all those years ago at the top of our cobblestone street in Atiquizaya when I told her we were moving to Santa Ana was the first bead in a necklace of losses. Then came Lauro; Marlene, my best friend in Santa Ana; Pati and Rebeca, our neighbors in Santa Ana; teachers who were my parents' friends and whom I also knew; the houses and the trees in those houses whom I'd befriended and would never see again. Our losses were compounded by the terrible knowledge that we were moving to places farther and farther away. The day we left El Salvador my family knew that for us there was no possibility of a real return. Mami and Papá had painstakingly given away all of our furniture, appliances—even the new sewing machine Mami had recently bought. Papá's beloved books, my own library, our toys, most of our clothes, cooking utensils, dishes, we left all of it behind, even our dear pets, Monina and Frederick, knowing our departure was final and that a return was a distant possibility.

It would have been more genuine and more satisfactory to submit as my assignment a series of questions:

Is home a structure?

Is it a place? Is it people?

What if home is country?

Or does home have to be a shelter—a physical place?

What if home was trust between family members? What did home sound like when you'd lost your ability to speak your pain and your fears?

Could home be language?

Could one be a home in oneself?

Can home be a memory?

We—my family and I—worked hard to obliterate any trace that may reveal the pain in the realization that what we left behind is forever lost. We worked hard, for decades, to suppress the terror of the war we survived. But the terror never left. It only simmered under the new lives we built. Each member of my family who left El Salvador during those years carries within them a piece of the puzzle that was the war: the dead, the tortured, the exiled, the displaced, the disappeared, the trafficked, those who remained. But not one of my family members has ever really spoken about the colors, textures, sounds, and feelings their puzzle piece contains.

Is the recognition of our loss the same for each of us? Can we, each of us, agree on a common version of our exile? Or are our feelings and memories arranged so differently as to not recognize one another's versions of things?

The old house in Atiquizaya is the receptacle where my mind has deposited a feeling of safety and wellbeing. It appears in moments when I seek reassurance. The more I call upon its image for solace, the more I don't see the imperfections and shortcomings I experienced when we lived there, such as the lack of potable water and sewage infrastructure. The more I idealize its image, the more the idea of an idyllic time ossifies in my mind.

Exile forces that. It distorts things. Filters them. Exile creates parity with our longing. When that which we long for in the old country does not match the reality of what we lived, we remember it each time a little differently and each time we blur the edges of the unpleasant details. We do it until we are left with the unblemished image of that which brings us comfort.

It is a way of surviving.

It is a way of surviving.

Six years after arriving in the US, my parents rented a condominium. We had rented apartments until then and sometimes shared spaces with family members. When we arrived in Florida, we shared a house with Tía Maura. When we arrived in California, we lived with my father's sister, Gina, her husband, their three children, and Abuela, who had come to the US to help Tía Gina with her three young sons. We were two families squeezed into a small two-bedroom house. We children slept with our abuela in the garage, which had been semi-converted into a bedroom. My tía's husband, Edgardo, installed a television set for Abuela to watch her beloved telenovelas. When the last telenovela of the day ended at 10 P.M., Abuela turned off the light and all of us miraculously fell asleep. She adhered to her routine even in this unlikely situation. Her actions showed us how to persevere. She protected our slumber, all of us sleeping, inhaling her fierce love.

The condo that my parents eventually afforded had a narrow-covered porch with a small patch of soil to the right of the front door, and there Papá squeezed a mano de león, a shade-tolerant plant that over time grew lush with large, waxy green leaves, deeply carved as to resemble a lion's paw. In the two-inch-wide sliver of dirt between the concrete and the redwood fence, Papá put in seeds, mostly radish. Between struggle and the fence, the ersatz of our beating hearts. These plants operated as memory placeholders, reminders of elsewhere and of the way we were.

With nothing other than a sixth sense, roots plunge toward their dark north single-mindedly, the way branches claim heaven. The fruit hang in the space of tension created by both poles. So it is with us immigrants, longing for what we left behind, and at the same time trying to birth new fruit in our new homes. We hope for a new harvest from our in-between place, one that contains the "there" and the "here." Often, we first broadcast our arrival, and resilience, through celluloid codes. I delight in driving or walking through immigrant neighborhoods, saluting the plants from elsewheres that often thrive in driveways and makeshift plant containers.

I've watched Papá prepare the ground to put in seeds or plant a young seedling as far back as I can remember; turning earth over for the new crop of corn he put in every year, making deep holes for this or that tree, putting in bare root roses. For Papá, digging, shoveling, fertilizing, and weeding were more than menial tasks. Gardening was primordial, a search, a hope, an anchoring—the incomparable smell of earth, freshly turned—a kind of magic encounter, a certainty that needed no words. For me and for him, gardening is a way of giving and receiving love. Gardening, and being among plants, is how I ground myself, and in some fashion, it is also my way to remember and reenact my papá's love.

20

Make Room for the New

Oakland, California, 2004

As I made progress with Noreen I also didn't give up on my efforts to find a new house. John acknowledged my efforts and even came along with me sometimes to view properties. I wanted him to fall in love with one of the houses we visited, or at least find a redeeming quality in one of them, but like a well-tempered clavier he clicked his objections to every house we toured: too expensive and overrated, too close to a freeway overpass, negligible backyard, too steep a lot, too far from downtown, not a good location to ride a bike to work.

One day we visited a beautiful, if unconventional, home in the Oakland Hills. The house was situated on a sloped lot; it had three stories, and each extended into the hill by way of generous decks. The large south-facing windows in each room made the entire house sing with light. The backyard was steep, but the owners had terraced it all the way down to where a pair of sequoias stood and the lot flattened. On each terrace, they had built vegetable beds and created small moments to enjoy the landscaping and the view.

I loved the house immediately. Yes, it was not practical—we'd have to be careful while the kids were still young—but I envisioned us enjoying the large pristine picture windows and light-filled rooms. As we rolled from the hilly part of town back to our house in the flats, my thoughts wandered back to the day of the shooting. Once again I saw our single-paned living room windows broken, glass shards strewn on the sunny rug. I considered how those wayward bullets broke my house and broke me too. After my visits with Noreen, I understood that living in a new house would no doubt help me, but in the back of my mind I sensed that my emotional, spiritual, and psychological hurt preceded the Oakland shooting. Nevertheless, driving home and in a chatty mood, I began listing the advantages and possibilities of the property we'd just seen. John listened.

"So, what do you think?" I asked eagerly once we were back home.

"Did you notice the way the decks were built?" he retorted. "Shoddy construction. Whoever built the house used the wrong screws."

Ugh. He found something unacceptable with every place we saw.

There were times when I agreed with some of his objections. I did like our house, after all. We had poured love, sweat, and tears into making it a comfortable and even charming place. I liked our neighbors. I just did not like the corner of Dover and Aileen.

"Why don't we switch realtors?" he finally said one day. "I feel that Gloria is not showing us houses best suited for us."

"Okay," I said, relieved that he was not giving up on searching altogether. "Who might be better? Any ideas?" I asked. In reality, I didn't care who we worked with. When he suggested the realtors on the corner of 51st and College Avenue, I agreed without reservation. "I'll make an appointment tomorrow," I said.

Within a week we sat across from Seth, a thirty-something with a high degree of confidence.

"The first thing we need to do is have your current house appraised," Seth said, "I have an excellent person for that. Once we have those figures, it will be easier for us to narrow choices."

John shifted in his seat at the suggestion. I know, because I know him, that everything about Seth's demeanor, including his straightforward way of doing business, grated him. Since our graduate student days at UCLA, John had dedicated his professional life to being an affordable housing advocate. Despite their tall, fit, blue-eyed exteriors, Seth and John were the inverse of each other. Where one was slick, the other was earnest; and where one saw a profit margin, the other understood housing for its use value.

"I hate realtors," John said as we made our way to our car.

Then the day arrived when an inspector came to appraise our house.

"Can you believe that?" I said to John when he came home that evening. He looked saddened by the news.

"You know this house is not worth $500,000, Claudia. That is absurd," he said.

I stared at him, knowing what he said was true. Every day newspapers reported on predatory lending.

"True. But it means we can afford to buy another house," I said, with defiance in my voice.

"If this house is appraised that high, just think how overpriced houses will be in the neighborhoods you want to live in!" John said.

We had gone over the same points endless times. Why couldn't John at least pretend to understand my position?

21

Sideways

Oakland, California, 1998

Six years before the shooting, John and I had made an offer on the small house with gray vinyl siding located between Aileen and 56th Streets. We had been living in the Bay Area for a few months, sleeping on friends' sofas, lining up house-sitting gigs while scouring the rental market in Oakland and Berkeley. We'd joined a paid rental listing service and toured dozens of apartments, small houses, attached cottages, and condos. We submitted plenty of applications and were outbid every time. In a eureka moment born of desperation we decided to look at fixer-uppers. The television show by that name didn't come out until many years later.

All the houses we looked at were in decidedly struggling neighborhoods. We drove and walked the streets around each of the listings that interested us. Chain-link fences were a common feature. We'd park in front of the house in consideration and imagine ourselves living there. We found a small cottage with gray vinyl siding on Dover Street in North Oakland and returned to it a few times. One evening as the sun went down, sitting in the cabin of John's dented Toyota Tacoma, across from the neglected house, we decided to make an offer on it. The house was small, on a flat lot, close to the Temescal neighborhood, with easy access to public transportation. At that particular moment I was unemployed, and John had a part-time gig at a housing nonprofit—which in a few years he would lead to great success. A mixture of hope, the need for shelter, and the appeal of fixing a home together welled up in us, and the next day, side by side, nervous and buoyed by optimism, we walked into the homegrown real estate firm on the corner of Shattuck and 51st across from Bushrod Park and placed our offer.

John and I had moved up to the Bay Area from Los Angeles, where we'd met on the first day of our graduate program in Urban Planning at UCLA. By coincidence, as such things go, we had each independently met one of only three foreign students in the program that year. I befriended a woman from Peru and John, a man from Costa Rica. On the first day, when the entire graduate cohort gathered for orientation, the international students sought one another out and John and I naturally gravitated toward the one person we each knew. This is how the four of us ended up sitting together in the auditorium to hear the director's welcoming address. I went into the row of seats first, John last. A round of introductions were made. I leaned way forward to offer my hand to the man sitting on the far side of our group. When our hands locked I felt an electric spark that matched the electricity of the eyes and smile of the man I was meeting for the first time. I was smitten. But whatever romantic thoughts I'd had that afternoon, I quickly abandoned them as John did not appear to reciprocate the same interest. We became friends instead.

There were late nights of writing, designing, and producing joint projects, hours and hours of discussing readings, pouring over census data sets, and mastering mapping software. We got along so well we decided to move in together with Guillermo, a dear friend of mine from my undergraduate days who was in his second year of law school at UCLA. Guillermo scouted an art deco three-bedroom duplex for us in the heart of Mid-Wilshire, and once settled in, we established what approximated a routine. John rode his bicycle to and from campus and I hopped in my mechanically challenged, sky-blue Lynx. Often, we would find each other in Lu Valle Commons at the end of the day to strategize dinner. So it went, oatmeal and apples in the morning courtesy of John and a meal prepared by me in the evening. Guillermo would now and then hop on for dinner, but mostly he kept busy with his own doings at the law school.

One evening toward the end of our time at UCLA John agreed to my offer to take a break from our studies and walk to a local bar for a late-night whiskey. At midnight I knocked on his bedroom door and pointed to my armband watch. He was reluctant to leave his desk, but I stressed that an agreement was an agreement. We walked over to the intersection of Wilshire and Olympic to our local bar. Soon we were lost in conversation, laughing, and teasing each other with the ease that had grown between us. Another couple sat a few stools away from us and we commiserated that the man seemed to be trying too hard to charm the woman.

We struck up a conversation with them. It turned out the couple were married, from Mexico City, and employed in different aspects of the film industry. When the bar closed at 2 A.M., we invited them to continue the banter at our place for another round. When they left our apartment at close to five in the morning, John and I collapsed side by side on our sofa. Something bloomed between us during our evening outing and that night marked the end of our friendship and the beginning of our romance. At that point, five weeks separated us from our master's degrees, and we worked hard to stay the course because everything became less important than spending time with each other.

Months earlier John had signed a lease with a friend on a house in the Bay Area, but once we became a couple, he backed out of the arrangement to stay in Los Angeles after graduation. In July the two of us left our Mid-Wilshire duplex to rent a small two-bedroom house next to a mature oak tree in the heart of Echo Park. We painted rooms and bought patio furniture. John ran extra outlets for computers and desk lamps in the second bedroom and built us desks by recycling old doors placed on sawhorses. I took a job at a union local, and he joined a special city taskforce to overhaul the rental code enforcement program for the city of Los Angeles. We were happy together, but by the end of a year John longed to return to the Bay Area, where he had lived before moving to LA to attend grad school, and I, having dear friends there, agreed to follow him north.

Then, a few days after placing our offer and after months of living out of backpacks, we received a phone call informing us that our bid to purchase the house on Dover Street had been accepted. It was the only bid the house received. We'd placed it on the last day the house was listed. Our spirits soared; our smiles could not be contained. We procured a loan by outsmarting the loan officer, whose misgivings might as well have been flashing off his forehead. We projected the confidence our graduate degrees from UCLA granted us. The officer gave in and approved a thirty-year mortgage loan.

The morning we received the keys to the house we drove straight there and, with elan and ceremony, uncorked a champagne bottle and smudged the house with sage. We knew it was going to take a lot of elbow grease to make the house pleasantly inhabitable. We knew, but didn't really know anything. In the kitchen a slight shove of the refrigerator sent hundreds of cockroaches skittling every which way for cover. We looked at each other and without a saying a word, unplugged, then pushed and shimmied the lumbering machine until we had it in the backyard. The stove followed, then the two layers of linoleum, cabinets, counters, even the kitchen sink.

We were spooked by the roaches and did not stop to consider what the dismantlement would cost us. In the following days, we pulled carpets, removed tack strips and, in the boldest move of all, completely gutted the bathroom. We removed the large claw-foot tub, sink, toilet, floor, and subfloor and tore the bathroom walls down from the wainscoting to the studs because we'd noticed rotting. Full of hubris, we did not stop to consider the weeks of living without a shower or a working toilet ahead of us. In the kitchen, John built a makeshift counter and dropped a sink into it. We made do without a functioning shower by bathing in the kitchen. Over the drilled Masonite panels that were our temporary kitchen flooring we placed thick water-resistant mats and painter's cloth, then set the largest galvanized bucket we could find on top. One of us sat in the bucket while the other poured water gently overhead. Bathing like this after a day's labor was not so bad; we took turns in the bucket, telling each other jokes and nothing stories, letting our laughter cascade like fresh, clean, water over our heads.

Once a week we drove over to Piedmont Springs and enjoyed a hot soak and a decent shower. In the backyard shed, we set up a bucket behind a couple of the doors we took from the house and used it as a pee toilet. For larger needs we relied on our neighborhood: the public library, local restaurants, and coffee shops. November arrived and for my birthday, in a cheeky gesture, John gifted me a new toilet bowl. I was elated, but we were still weeks away from having a fully renovated bathroom.

In the meantime, we found tradespeople to replace the house's decaying plumbing and the old knob-and-tube electrical wiring. Others sanded and restained the wood floors. We painted the rooms in cheerful colors. The day we no longer needed to cover the bed with a plastic sheet to protect it from dust was the day I felt we finally moved in. I drew a postcard of the house and collaged a picture of Toby, my rescue pug, in front of the drawing. I proudly mailed it with our new address to friends and family. A year and a half later we were married, and a year after that Aurora was born. We did not have a master, a ten-year, or a five-year plan. We were simply living.

22

Everything Has Its Story

Oakland, California, 2004

Even as I began to see benefits of working with Noreen, there were plenty of times when I felt like I had nothing left to unpack. I told myself I was fine; I didn't need her help anymore. Some days, I devised elaborate exit strategy scenarios: *What if Edith rings and says Aurora has a stomach bug?*

Despite my negativity, I also learned to put feelings and thoughts as they unfolded during the week in the Noreen bucket. Nothing was left out of our conversations: work, the civil war, John, my parents, Oakland, my desire to write.

I squeezed out the incident in front of the house until there was nothing left—not a drop of water remained in its wrung-out shape. It needed to be that way. It took months for me to be able to even look at the stop sign on the corner of Aileen and Dover. The day I walked over and stood next to the stop sign, I knew I'd made some progress. Even though my thoughts played out dire scenarios anytime a group of youths walked in my direction, I learned to control my flight instinct. I was able to remain calm and understand no one was out there to kill me or ambush me.

With practice, I also learned to let emotion come. Memories. Dreams. I watched their approach, withstood their ambush. My resistance lessened and the waves crashed and crashed inside my widening self, and I let them. I let them erode, scrape, and reshape the contours of myself. I knew in forty minutes' time, I would get up from the brown sofa, thank the angels in heaven, la Virgen, y todos los Santos for the rear exit door, go home, fix dinner, and still have energy to brush my teeth before collapsing into bed rather than onto the floor or at the dinner table, as was often the case when I first started seeing Noreen.

If silver linings exist, then the shooting in front of my house is the glittering, single event that catapulted me into becoming a writer. Until then I had always wanted to write but did not know how to go about it, and I did not yet have the words to name what I felt. I had too many fears about writing: Would what I had to say be of value or good enough? Would anyone want to read it? I let doubt prevent me from trying. The shooting took care of that. I was so confused by the feelings and memories that surfaced in the aftermath that the only thing I could think to do was write and it didn't matter whether what I wrote was any good or if anyone would ever read it.

The shooting in front of the house unleashed a thirst for anything that helped me explain to myself the dislocation I felt. How did I come to be here? How is it that my only response after the shooting was to want to run away, to abandon the house? In the reflecting pool of the aftermath, I saw a person I could hardly recognize. Or I could not see the person I understood myself to be. For years I had been living a double life. The life of my body in the world, parting air as I walked, making sounds when I spoke, and the life beneath my skin, a river of blood flowing through vein and artery, and coiling in its current, memories and a second language. A potent language: flor, mar, tierra.

Unfortunately for my writing aspirations, years of schooling and attending universities in the United States and abroad, the diplomas and certificates I'd earned, the very things I credited with making me successful, also nourished in me a kind of alienation. My love of literature, rather than encouraging my efforts, instilled a lack of trust in my own abilities and in my own stories, in my family's stories. The literature classes I took in college emphasized criticism, not creative output. In classes we scrutinized writers considered masters of world literature; what chance was there for the type of writing I might want to do? Reading and writing were split from each other, when in fact they play off each other, they work in tandem. My internalized fears and oppressions made me question what, if anything, could I possibly contribute to any literary landscape?

When Izal was about to turn a year old, I signed up for my first creative writing class, not knowing what I wanted to get out of it, not knowing what to expect, and without any understanding as to why I was signing up in the first place. All I knew was that I had to do it. To my surprise, the class I chose at the local community college was well attended, each desk taken, even those at the very front and those at the very back of the room. For some of the students the course was an item to be ticked off the list of graduation requirements, for others the creative outlet was a kind of salvation.

Working with Noreen was helping me understand and face my fears, but increasingly so were my writing classes at Laney College in Oakland. I looked forward to the evenings when class was held, relished listening to others read their compositions, and worked diligently to create my own. Step-by-step over the course of those classes I began to understand that writing is like air: accessible to everyone. When I was a college student, and maybe even earlier in my life, I had wished to write, but the authors I read pointed me away from my aspiration. For one thing, I encountered more male than female authors, but even the female authors I read in my college classes were shrouded in mystery and did not reflect my reality as an immigrant Central American young woman learning English. What I gathered was that writing happened to other people—not to people like me.

As a child, I had felt the tug of writing. And I did write, on notebooks pages or on other surfaces. In the fourth grade, playing during school recess, I fell backward off a ledge. The impact forced all air from my lungs, and for the few minutes I struggled to fill myself back up with air, I was rendered speechless. The experience terrified me. I opened my mouth, and nothing came out, not a word, not even the raspiest croak. I ran to the main office seeking help but when I tried to speak my mouth uttered only silence. I thought I had lost my ability to speak, but gradually, as my lungs reinflated, my voice returned. That afternoon, safely at home, I wrote the story down on the white cotton slip I'd been wearing underneath my uniform. I still have it. My young, globular handwriting sprawled over the white undergarment in blue ink, forcing it to bear witness to my fright. I even titled the story "Esta conbinación tiene su historia," meaning, "This slip has its own history." Writing the experience down taught my young self that things, plants, and animals, like people, also have stories to tell.

Ever so slowly, the classes at the community college demystified writing for me. I learned that writing has to do with sharing one's thoughts, doubts, fears, desires. It is not something mysterious; it does not require a university degree. Everyone has feelings, everyone has stories to share. I learned that writing requires both heart and mind. The craft of writing is one thing, the heart of writing another. Perhaps the most important thing I learned was that much of writing is editing and perseverance. The craft of writing needs to be learned, like baking a cake, driving a car, or operating a lawn mower.

Like a good seed, I took to writing's terrain, but the ground had already been tilled for years. As far back as elementary school, the classroom had always been a space of belonging for me, a beloved space. Something beginning with the geometric arrangement of desks in a room, the individual seats holding the body safely while my mind entered a garden of language and ideas. This is not to deny that classrooms can be oppressive and mind-numbing. I have had searing experiences in them, yet my desire for learning made it so I would bring myself to the classroom each day with anticipation for what new flower I might harvest.

I loved my first creative writing class but my devotion to learning was instilled in me much earlier by both of my parents. Mami gave me the world twice. She granted me light at birth and then again when she taught me to read and write. I ran away from kindergarten when I was four years old. "It's all good," my parents said. *It's all good*, I told myself, because the only thing I loved about school were the small bananas drizzled with honey served as midmorning snack.

To four-year-old Claudita some of the teachers were unpleasant, but Doña Carlota, the buxom white-haired caretaker, was downright mean. One day, when I saw the big wooden doors open, I simply walked out. I strolled around the corner where I knew my cousin's father worked in a shop that sold fertilizers and pesticides. Don Dagoberto assigned me to a chair in the corner of the shop and told me to wait while he sent word home that I was with him.

"No matter," both my parents said. Over lunch, Mami declared that she was going to teach me to read and write instead. A few days later a school desk arrived at the house, and every afternoon, after she came home after teaching fifth grade at an all-boys school, I took my place behind the desk's kidney-shaped arm, and she showed me how to make magic by pairing vowels to consonants. After a few lessons, I was stringing together stars and suns, flowers and birds, making them trot and fly and sing. I was a quick study. Who needed kindergarten, or Doña Carlota?

A decade later, I was fourteen and attending high school in West Palm Beach, Florida. Bilingual education and other programs to help newcomer students like me were nonexistent at this school at that time. I spent my days trying to stay afloat in a sea of English, holding on to my life ring—a Spanish–English dictionary. I moved from class to class, understanding only a handful of words, except in my math and Spanish lessons. In the math classroom I could easily follow arithmetic and algebra assignments. Numbers are numbers. In the Spanish class the teacher was Cuban and full of candor and kindness. She made me TA. I was suddenly grading other tenth-grade students' homework and quizzes, and that gesture gave me a great deal of confidence. In her class, I was myself, chatting in Spanish with a fluent speaker who was also an immigrant.

When Papá was not at work washing dishes at the seafood restaurant on Military Trail, he sat with me to help me decipher my homework and reading assignments, which were all in English. He translated out loud what he could while I looked for unknown words in the dictionary. He taught me to keep a glossary of the words we identified and so I filled a notebook with columns of words and their translations. On my own, I went back and read and reread my notebook to memorize the words and their meanings. With him as my guide, I learned to notice and appreciate the contour of words, their length, their architectures, the thingness of them. Here we were tending a different kind of garden, planting seeds that would eventually become written compositions—the flowers and trees of my mind.

At Laney College, in the noncompetitive environments the professors created, I found my way back to El Salvador, and into my happy place: Atiquizaya. Words showed up, opening roads to places long forgotten. Over the blank page, I chased the world of color I knew as a child, bird and road, smile and dream, house and metaphor. Like a pied piper, I called forth words with the music of my pen from the nooks and crannies of my body, and the sleeping words that I'd carried inside me for years responded. First, I wrote of my immediate family, and slowly, I spiraled outward to tell of the streets, the sky, the barrio and, eventually, my first country, the country of our birth. Looking back on this creative time, I understand I was writing a compendium of the people and the places that held me when I was in El Salvador and that hold me to this day. It is on their foundation that I live.

23

Dulce

Atiquizaya, El Salvador 1972 / El Monte, CA 1994 / Oakland, CA, 2004

I'd always enjoyed my abuela's company, her brashness, and her unabashed, round, radish sting of a laugh. She returned to me unbidden, sometimes during my conversations with Noreen. Slowly I came to understand the force and blessing my abuela is to me now as a spirit and the influence she had on me when she was alive.

Abuela was one of five children. Her two sisters died in adulthood, leaving young children behind, while Abuela and her two brothers survived into old age. She married a slender man, my father's father, who would soon die from a brain complication. My papá was three years old. Abuela never married again but had a relationship with a married man with whom she had two daughters eighteen months apart. For this, she was punished. Her parents mistrusted her and took Papá away from her. Before this misfortune happened, her mother had taught her the secrets to candy making. On her own, Abuela survived selling jams, jellies, and conservas—traditional sweets made from a variety of sugars and fresh fruit. No fruit or vegetable escaped her culinary gift. She turned oranges, figs, mangoes, tamarinds, watermelon, and squashes into succulent confections. She roasted and ground cacao beans and hand-rolled the powder into chocolate tablets.

To enter her house was to enter an alchemist's lab. Baskets brimmed with seasonal fruits; sacks of raw cocoa beans and white, turbinado, and panela sugars leaned against the narrow space in front of the courtyard that led to the dark backroom. If the fruit did not get turned into candy quickly enough, swarms of flies would descend to gorge on the flesh and imbibe their sugars.

Unlike our verdant courtyard, hers was a gaping mouth that flooded the corridor with light, while the other rooms in the house marinated in shadows. In this modest space, my abuela manifested her alchemist powers. Here she took base ingredients—fruit, nuts, sugar—and converted them into candies and conservas that were the gustatory synthesis of our tropical terroir. In her hands the flesh of coconuts mixed with molasses became rhomboid-shaped morsels that made me shimmy with a skip. She made her confections based on recipes passed down orally by her mother and grandmother, but she injected into them her spicy wits.

Every day green coconuts were delivered to her house and piled in the otherwise empty courtyard. When the sun eased its grip, Tío Samuel—Abuela's brother and Lauro and Cornelia's father—showed up and, deploying his stellar machete technique, slashed hundreds of cocos. Sitting on a low three-legged stool, he slashed their tops, drained their milk into a bucket, whacked them in half, then into quarters. Thus, the coconuts awaited the next person who would scoop out the white meat for yet another set of hands to chop and dice for my abuela to turn into the conservas she sold in Chalchuapa's market.

In the middle of this space, halfway covered by the corridor, was a firepit Abuela had ordered custom-made. Every afternoon, a local kid, looking to earn a few coins, would build and stoke a ferocious fire. On it would go a huge black cauldron filled with sugar and raw fruit that would become the day's conservas. I stood nearby many times to watch the alchemy happen. Coconut cubes and raw brown sugars liquefied then boiled under the hell stoked beneath. Flames lapped up the side of the cauldron, making me recall the painting of an inferno at the side entrance of the church in Atiquizaya. I could see, in my mind's eye, the naked bodies twisting in agony, engulfed by fiery tongues, their faces screaming, cowering and, most of all, regretting.

The cauldron was hoisted onto the roaring pit and Abuela handed any of us short people hovering nearby a long paddle and ordered us to stir. The paddle needed to be very long because the moment the boiling, spitting sugar touched the skin of an unlucky stirrer, a grotesque, opaque bubble formed. Any one of us who had lived through the pain of such a blister did the stirring carefully and in earnest.

When the sugars roiled and reached their boiling point, the contents of the cauldron were poured over a majestic table nearly the length of the corridor and left to harden overnight. The next day, using a long knife, Abuela cut the conservas into rhomboid shapes. The cut pieces sat for an entire day, left to cure, before being packaged into the baskets she took to the market. When darkness fell, work shifted to the windowless back room. Three or four women, depending on the day, surrounded by the smell of sugars, coconut, and cocoa, sat with low baskets on their knees, trimming and dicing the coconut flesh, which had been scooped out from their hairy shells earlier in the day.

A bare light bulb hung from the exposed rafters and the television's glare inundated the space. A parade of telenovelas ensued and the women, hands chopping away, would go in and out of plots, comparing the telenovelas' twists and turns to their own lives.

"Dígame, niña."

"Ay, no."

"Pues sí."

Abuela's house hummed with life. If everyone in the back room working those evenings had been a firefly the house would have blazed with the collective energy of everyone's throbbing lights.

My abuela must have been lonely all those years back in El Salvador, handling so many decisions, orchestrating employees, keeping bank records on her own. Her temper was the wall she hid behind to keep people at bay. If she was not bitter, it was because she was endowed with a wicked sense of humor and profound faith. Her harshness and brashness were the result of having known very little kindness. Too bad few understood the magnitude of her accomplishment. And too bad that by the time I came into this understanding she was sick, and I lived miles away from her and could not drop in to hold her hand, comb her hair, be blessed by her laughter.

When I moved to the Bay Area, Abuela lived in suburban Los Angeles, where she spent her days mostly alone in a big house. She had arrived in the United States to help her youngest daughter, Tía Gina, who had immigrated in the 1970s, with her two young sons. Abuela looked after the boys while Tía tended her fledging Salvadoran restaurant. The boys grew. One went off to college; the other moved out on his own. The one restaurant became two bustling establishments. Over time Abuela's help—taking kids to school, preparing meals—was no longer needed and her own days of hustling to keep her own candy-making business afloat were long behind her.

She was older and weaker, and her luster was no longer what it once was. But she still laughed her full belly laugh and used the same irreverent language. "¡Chimado! ¡Venga para acá!" "¡Hijoeputa!" "¿Qué mierdas son estas?" She sprinkled her days, and ours, with "shits," "whores," "asses." Or worse. Most importantly, she had not lost her spiritual compass. She kept a variety of saint images to which she attached little bundles of herbs and incense. She still wore a scapular doused in holy water around her neck and still left a glass of water by her bed overnight to ensure that her soul would never go thirsty and would find her way back into her now-aging body.

Whenever I visited her in LA, we sat together on her bed and watched the telenovela du jour. It was comforting, probably more for me than for her, to sit next to each other, laugh, and hold our breaths in unison at the unfolding action. Alzheimer's skulked in her already and it was disheartening to see my once dynamic, tempestuous Abuela relegated to a stuffy room, spending long hours without a person to talk to.

Those telenovelas are all the same. Once you've seen one you've seen them all, and she had seen hundreds over the years. But the point was not the telenovela, but rather the comfort of the familiar. What carried her were the memories of when she was a boss and the screen afforded levity after a day's hard labor and mental strain. In Los Angeles we watched telenovelas on Canal 34. What remained unsaid between us was held in place by delicate memories like the aroma and taste of sweet coconut water poured from a freshly cut fruit, the way it had been in the adobe courtyard of a house in Atiquizaya long ago.

If I visited Abuela on a Sunday, then I'd drive her to Our Lady of Guadalupe Church in nearby El Monte to hear mass in Spanish. For an hour we entered a borderless space: the brown faces, the Spanish spoken at the altar and by everyone around us, the guitar chords from the musical group, all emanated a beloved familiarity. For that hour, next to Abuela, I was home. The rest of the time I was dislocated: My body was in California, my mind unsure of itself, and my heart bravely trying to fit in.

As Abuela's Alzheimer's became pronounced, her three children, Tía Gina, Tía Valeria, and Papá, decided it was best for her to live out her days in El Salvador. She would return to the street where she had been born, to the house where I'd grown up and that now belonged to Tía Valeria.

"Venite ya," Papá said over the telephone. Come immediately. "Abuela is dying. If you want to see her alive once more, the time is now," he said with urgency in his voice.

"¡Ya!"

That same afternoon I flew from San Francisco's airport to Los Angeles and at midnight boarded a plane for San Salvador. Nine hundred miles later I found her in the same house, in the same room where I had grown from a baby to a school-aged child. She was lying down. Her old, tired face and smooth brow resting on a white pillowcase. Her emaciated body was so light and frail she could float off the bed. If I closed my eyes, I could see the layout of the room when I was a small child. My salmon-pink bed stood in the corner next to the single window whose big wooden shutters now let in just enough light, and a wedge of azure sky, to illuminate her pale, papery-thin skin.

In the room was Papá, Tía Valeria, and Telma from across the street. Abuela was rarely ever alone in the old house. Someone was nearby, ready to take care of her needs. Neighbors sometimes poked their head in just to ask how she was doing that particular morning or afternoon. She had grown much older since I'd last seen her. And she was gaunt. The weight she once carried, and which gave her laughter a hearty, sonorous bite, was gone. The weight loss had taken away the material woman she had been and with it her memories and concerns. There was no worry, anxiety, or joy polluting her face. Without our memories we are not ourselves. Each event in our life is a silvery thread in a spider's web: the tension that holds us together. With no mooring my abuela began to dissolve, on her way to dust, skin and bones.

She did have moments, slivers of lucidity. One of them ignited her mind when I walked into the room and made my way to her bedside. "¡Aquí estás!" she said. After so many years of not being in each other's presence, she recognized me. I sat next to her, held her hand, touched her face; I was there with her. I was there next to her.

I stayed for a week. Abuela did not have another lucid moment with me even though I seldom left her side. One afternoon, I asked Tía Valeria to take me to the local open-air market to purchase flowers. I returned to her bedside with an armful of red roses like the ones the Virgin of Guadalupe conjured for Juan Diego atop Tepeyac Hill. My abuela deserved all the roses in the world and if she had been more herself, she would have loved the gesture. The two of us were huge fans of rose-scented anything: soaps, perfumes, creams. I stepped into the darkened room where she lay, and the flower's fragrance filled the space, but she did not react in any way; even after I'd told her where I'd been and what I'd brought.

Abuela died a week after my return to California. Tía Valeria left her bedside for a moment, Papá recounted, and when she returned Abuela was gone. Camila Vargas lived a full, long, life. She was surrounded by people who loved her and cared for her, people whom she loved in turn. I learned from my papá the details of her wake, funeral mass, burial, and subsequent nine days of prayers. On Día de los Muertos—Día de Finados for us in El Salvador—relatives visit her gravesite, clean it, and bring her flowers. We call this enflorar, to enflower, which is to love, to remember.

Whenever I visit El Salvador I make sure to spend time at her gravesite. I take her flowers, wash the tiles that cover her grave and the inside of the minuscule chapel that Tía Valeria built for her. Papá and Tía Valeria are usually with me. We sit, make small talk, tell family stories. I like to take in the play of shadows, hear the tussling of leaves among the abundant trees. More than a somber place, the cemetery in Atiquizaya resembles a colorful village. The resting place of its citizens reflects the town that the living inhabit and the unorthodox way the town has evolved over time. Gravesites resist uniformity and nod either to the deceased's personality or the tastes and economic circumstances of their surviving relatives. Graves are also crammed next to one another, leaving little space to navigate around them. The cemetery's entrance has a few ornate and grand gravesites that have been painted white, with chapels sporting ornate wrought iron doors. Elsewhere, cherubs flank elaborate headstones. Farther inside the cemetery, graves become more and more eclectic. Some are covered in bright tiles with headstones featuring mosaics depicting a particular saint or la Virgen de Guadalupe. Some are quiet and modest, and others still are mounds of dirt anchored with a wooden cross.

It was on one of these visits to Abuela's gravesite that I learned that Glenda's own burial place was nearby. After Glenda sought refuge in our house in San Salvador, when she trembled at any nighttime sound, I never saw her again. Glenda quietly passed away in Atiquizaya. Unlike Yuri, who married and started a family, Glenda was never able to overcome the demons that took hold of her during the war. From our house she returned to her parents' home and stayed there until her death. Don Galo died while Glenda was still alive. Doña Elba was left alone in the house. Eventually mother and daughter were placed in the same grave. When I first visited their gravesite, I saw that the cross bore Doña Elba's full name and had dates marking her birth and death. Glenda was identified by first name only.

The war made of Glenda a half person. She was unable to recover the lust and joy for life she once had. That her resting place was marked by only part of her name broke my heart. I asked Tía Valeria if we could find someone to carve a headstone that listed both women with their full names and dates of birth and death. Tía Valeria agreed that it was a good idea. She spoke with Yuri to ask permission and my tía paid out of her own pocket for the materials and labor. My tía asked the carver to indicate that the gesture was a gift made by me to honor their memory.

Abuela, her two sisters, and her two brothers, died as people should: from old age, from their ailing bodies after having led active, productive lives. My great-grandmother and great-grandfather are buried not far from my abuela. Lauro is in another section buried underneath a generous tree. All of them rest while birds whistle tunes from lush tree branches, their music falling prettily onto their graves like lluvia de Mayo, good May rain.

These days, come November 2, I set an altar with my abuela's photograph on the top tier. I place sweets similar to the ones Abuela made at the foot of her photograph. I don't have photos of Lauro and Glenda, otherwise they would be present in that way. I place water, candles, incense, marigolds. I sit with John and our children in front of the altar, drinking chocolate caliente, eating pan de muerto, telling stories of our departed. We tell the same stories year after year so that our children can come to know their ancestors as if they had met them.

*

Whenever I get my hands on homegrown Roma tomatoes, I make tomato jam the way my abuela taught me. The seed of Alzheimer's was already planted in her body when she shared the recipe with me. She was living with Tía Gina and her then-teenage sons in her two-story house in the heart of Pomona, California. We made small talk sitting at the kitchen table as the sun beat down mercilessly, bleaching the yard on the other side of the glass doors. It was around 2 P.M. and she stood up to prepare us the obligatory cup of afternoon coffee. When she came back with the steaming mugs, she had with her two bowls with what she called dulce de tomate. I had never heard of, nor tasted, such a dish. The compote was still warm and emanated a delicious cinnamon-laced aroma. At the bottom of the bowls, the ruby flesh of the Romas glistened like royal hearts with the syrup she had ladled over them. Hesitantly, I took a small bite and was delighted: the meaty consistency of the tomatoes, their acidity, and the syrup in which they were cooked made a splendid combination.

I marveled, not for the first time, at my abuela's creativity and enterprise. She did not have at her disposal zapotes, mangoes, guavas, nances, the fruit she was used to poaching and transforming into candy. She did not have the requisite sweet bread or cookies at home to accompany coffee, so she utilized what was at hand: tomatoes. I don't know how often she'd made the confection; from my end she could have made it up that afternoon. I certainly had never eaten it in Atiquizaya. My abuela's body was weaker but her impulse to create gustatory beauty was irrepressible.

I asked for the recipe, and she dictated it on the spot. Nothing about it was exact. Get six or seven tomatoes, make an X with a sharp knife at both ends, put them in boiling water, and cover them, to let the steam loosen their skins. After a while remove the tomatoes, peel them, cut them in half. On a small pot, combine some sugar with water, add cinnamon, a squeeze of lemon juice, bring to a roaring simmer, drop the tomatoes in the hot syrup and cook quietly until done. I took notes, tried to pin down her vagueness: How much sugar? How do long do I let the compote simmer after the syrup boils?

The first time I tried the recipe on my own was a disaster. But after a few tries I managed something akin to her dulce. This unscientific method is how my abuela walked through life. It is how a single woman with three children built a successful business. She must have walked into many adversaries and into many walls and strayed into dead ends. The rejections she experienced taught her to never give up, to trust her intuition, to have unwavering faith. My abuela has been a kind of Beatrice in my life. She took me by the hand, as Beatrice led Dante into the inferno, and showed me in every way available to her how to grasp the world beneath the one my eyes perceive. In her inimitable way, she taught me to face the world with aplomb, to be cachimbona, a badass, like she was.

In the front garden of my house I tend a rue plant. Abuela taught me that this plant wards off evil spirits. I have planted rue in every place I've lived since the late 1990s. The plant I have now in front of my house struggles through the cold winter, but it flourishes in summer year after year. It too is a cachimbona. Growing up, I was surrounded by many cachimbona women: Glenda and Yuri, their mother, Lauro's mother. Women who walked facing the adversity of their days, making space for joy and time for prayer. I cut rue from my garden, place it on my altar; its pungent smell transports me to the realm of spirit, and I pay tribute to all the cachimbonas on whose shoulders I stand.

Visions of Gladness

I wish my grandmother's ghost
would gladden every day my slumber

her stardust halo, her luminous face—
by now I know fear both cages and unbinds.

Sometimes I hear her laughter
spiraling toward me like a kindly twister

fall in, she says, become not the rosary,
one bead in front of the other—

girl, woman, wife, mother, widow—
become pomegranate seeds instead

each jewel bursting forth from her own papery case
whirling in her own blood, by her own light charged.

She says this, and this is why, on my altar, as she taught me,
there is rue, incense, light, and water in a cup.

24

Flor y Canto

Oakland, California, 2005

It happened often that, when I set out to write a story for class, I ended up writing a poem. Words organized themselves into poetic verses before I knew what a line break was. Poetry came to choose me unbidden.

One day after class ended at Laney College, the young professor who taught our class asked me to linger for a minute. I could see he was holding a poem I'd written about my father and his garden in Atiquizaya. "I'd love you to read your poem at our next open mic," he said. Open mic? What was that? I'd never heard of an open mic. He explained that once a month in the college auditorium, creative writing students read their work to the school community and the general public. I trembled at the idea of reading one of my poems out loud. Professor Weidenbach reassured me that the reading was a safe and welcoming space. He also suggested I submit the poem for publication in Laney's creative writing magazine.

"My Father's Garden" is the first poem I ever read to an audience. When my name was called the day of the reading, my knees shook. I surprised myself when I walked onto the stage, stood under the beam that illuminated the podium, and recited my poem. Months later I read the poem again to a smaller audience at a reception in celebration of the latest edition of *Good News*, the school's journal. At the reception a person asked me to sign my name in her copy of the magazine next to my poem. I acquiesced, surprised by her request. She was a native of the city we lived in, did not speak Spanish, had never visited Central America. Yet something in my writing struck a chord with her. She related to what I had written. The incident underscored for me, as never before, that one of the miracles of the duality that is reading and writing is that when we read we inhabit other's proportions and concerns.

When I first started writing, gathering myself in front of one of my poems neatly printed on a clean sheet of paper ready for workshop surprised and delighted me. To see my experience reflected on the page widened me. My mind and body trusted the process ever more and yielded to the discoveries and awareness that come with writing. But even more important to me was the feeling that writing about El Salvador gave form to my family's experience of exile. Writing helped put in perspective El Salvador's history. Thousands of Salvadoran lives have been lost to government repression. Salvadorans, we were disposable pawns to the oligarchs, the military, and the United States, which conveniently dragged the human rights struggle of the Salvadoran people into a Cold War scenario to advance its geopolitical interests. My writing clamored to tell a story that was fully embodied and told from a Salvadoran point of view. For too long Salvadorans appeared as faceless people in news stories, stories written by some who did not carry the heat and sultriness of volcanic ash coursing through their veins.

For my fourth birthday, Mami crocheted a coral skirt of the finest linen thread. Designed with row upon row of perfectly shaped scallops, the skirt felt luxurious and heavy as I pulled it up to my waist, where it settled in a perfect fit. That year my birthday was on a Thursday and the gift made the occasion so perfect that I came to believe that all my birthdays had always been, and forever should be, on Thursdays. To revisit the perfection of that day, the surprise, the feeling of being so loved and cared for, is a difficult task. The memory lives unblemished, tucked in the remotest part of my brain, where bad things can't reach. To take it out of its quiet place and look at it is akin to stepping out on a perfect summer day with the sun ripe with benevolent glory only to feel its rays blind me with their force. I cannot hold the memory for long out of concern that my gaze will knock it out of the edges of its splendid frame.

That memory is a memory of my mother, of her love for me, and it is a memory of place. Writing out the memory, I could feel the sun on my face as I stood on the side of the house facing my father's rose garden, trying on the skirt for the first time. The skirt was the same salmon color as some of Papá's prized roses. Looking back, I was a small rose myself, un botón de rosa, a rose button, as we say in El Salvador. The mango tree witnessed my joy. It must have watched Mami crocheting it on the veranda when I was not around. That courtyard, to this very day, thrives with flowers and fruits from plants my parents planted when we lived in the house.

Places have their own vibrational force which seeps into us; they become part of us. Places change us—our body chemistry—but the places we inhabit hold on to us as well. We, with our presence and own vibrations and actions, change the places we inhabit. Places remember too. Some part of us, of my family, is still in that house where we lived so many happy, formative days. Camila and I spent our earliest childhoods protected by our parents, by the adobe walls, and by the leaves, flowers, and branches of the trees and shrubs that nurtured us with their beauty and kindness. We never fully left El Salvador. Part of us is still there, flowering away.

The summer before I went away to college, I worked at an organization, a day center, that provided opportunities for adults with developmental disabilities. I organized games, practiced manual dexterity drills, cleaned a chin or two, listened attentively to those whose mouths struggled to shape words intelligibly. One day at the staff lunch table, a woman sitting across from me told me, squarely to my face, to go back to where I came from. I stared back stunned. The comment arrested all conversation at the table for a hot second and in that silence, I thought if only she knew how much we didn't want to leave in the first place, and how it was her country that made mine the hell it became. My writing, arriving many years later, is my response to that comment.

My Father's Garden

Bears no resemblance
to the orderly paradises found
in glossy magazines
there are no tidy borders to admire
no coordinating color palettes
here the eye is overtaken
by mass of unapologetic green
olive green, forest green,
lemon green, green, green

And speckled among the verdor
calling attention to their resplendent selves
are flowers in many hues and shapes
the mallows, my father's favorites,
offer blooms as big as bird nests
petals glisten in mid-day sun
stretch wide and far
there is little modesty in their display

There is no coyness in this garden
only abundance and overflow
zinnias grow by the dozen
roses burst yellow, salmon, red
bougainvilleas, trumpet flowers
a pulsing profusion
planted all with trembling hands

Twenty exile years
is a long time to contemplate
each leaf
a coming to terms with lost ideals
each flower
a testament to fallen friends
each new seedling
a last salute to persecutions of the heart
my father's garden a nascent Eden
a rooting back to his native land.

25

A Door Opens

Oakland, California, 2004–2005

"I have good news for you," Seth told me when I answered the phone. After viewing countless houses that met our price range, he had found a house that met our criteria to a T. He was sure of it. I hung up the kitchen phone, its long cord almost touching the floor, and lingered at its side, enjoying the lightness that had suddenly flushed my body. Finally, the house I longed for had materialized, was available in Oakland. We scheduled a tour at John's earliest availability. On the appointed day I strapped the kids in their car seats, sat in the passenger seat, and looked John's handsome face squarely in the eye, as if to say, "We did it!" I enjoyed the drive to the vicinity of Lake Merritt, where the house was located, feeling as we drove that we were about to make our future home's acquaintance. As our van crested the hillock on which the house stood, we could see that Seth was already there, standing next to the For Sale sign, and in a flash he was on the front stoop, ready to open the door for us. But before I opened the car door, I knew this house was not for us.

On a block of nicely appointed houses this one exuded neglect and disrepair. The house was fenceless, already a problem for us with our young children, and the backyard exhibited nothing but tired grass patches. The smell of mildew assaulted us the moment we stepped inside. The biggest wall in the living room had floor-to-ceiling mirror panels adorned with gold filigree. A gaudy chandelier hung from a low ceiling. The shag carpet released tired, musty smells with every step we took. I did not need to see the rest of the house—at that front room I'd seen enough. But we diligently followed Seth around, listening to his pitch about all the possibilities this or that room afforded. I even went down to check out the forlorn backyard, whose only point of access was from the back of the house after going down a rickety set of stairs. For the duration of the tour John and I said not a word to each other. We could read each other's faces. After the walk through, we stood for a moment with Seth on the sidewalk next to the For Sale sign.

"Isn't it just what you are looking for?!" Seth said cheerfully.

John and I looked at each other. John spoke, listing his marginal objections. I knew that he would never bother to give Seth the time to explain his substantial ones. Seth countered each objection with eagerness that slowly gave way to fraying enthusiasm until his frustration with us and our process unveiled itself.

"Haven't you seen enough houses?" he snapped, and surprised himself at the crack showing through his starched collar and impeccable tie.

Seth believed that the location and price point of the house were perfect for us. But we knew what the remodel would entail. And we had a sober idea of what the costs would be. If we went ahead with the purchase, not only would we assume a substantial mortgage, but we'd have to borrow additionally to clean and repair the house and make it amenable for our family. From every financial angle, it made sense for us to stay in our own home. We had enough equity in it that we could borrow against it and remodel it in the way we had fantasized over the years—repair the crumbling foundation we meant to fix when we bought it, add a bedroom and a bathroom and dedicated office space. This, of course, had been John's argument all along.

I valued John's argument and on occasion I even agreed with it, but the fear of another shooting penned me in. Fear limits you. Chains you. Now, a year from the shooting incident and after months of working with Noreen, I could hold that thought, approach it with a degree of detachment. There was no guarantee that violence might not erupt again in our neighborhood. There was no gun safety guarantee anywhere, even in the toniest neighborhoods. I had witnessed enough drug deals in plain daylight in all kinds of neighborhoods across the city. Gun violence was a certainty in Oakland when we lived there. A shooting might erupt anytime, anywhere, even in schools. I finally could see that I was not random violence's only target. The way a moment of sunlight on an otherwise dull winter's day imparts rich luminescence upon treetops, with that kind of lucidity, I understood that the answer to overcoming my fear was not to move away. Running was not going to make the fear ever leave me because the fear lived inside me. The ordeal with Seth revealed that the only way to overcome my terror was to face it.

The disappointment with Seth forced a recalibration not only of my efforts to move but of our life in general. I gave up my job at the children's museum where I worked part-time when the cost of childcare became prohibitive. We decided that it was best for me to stay home with Izal and Aurora and take advantage of the many writing classes offered during the day instead of in the evenings. John continued to ride his red commuter bike to his nonprofit job in downtown Oakland. Our children grew stronger, more able, and more curious each day. Aurora started preschool while Izal and I took the mornings to visit parks, see friends and, once a week, walk over to the Temescal library where we read books together and listened to the children's librarian share stories and songs during the baby/toddler hour.

We didn't abandon the idea of moving. In fact, John thought that moving to another city altogether might be a better choice. I liked this idea very much. Of all the places we discussed, Portland rose to the top of our list. We had neighbors a block away moving there. We gathered intelligence from friends and acquaintances who had either grown up in Portland or had lived there.

It so happened that three of Mami's sisters were visiting the US at the same time we were thinking of a Portland move. My tías flew up to visit us and the children and we took advantage of their presence, time, and love of our kids to visit Portland on our own. My kids were too young and might never be able to recount the weekend they spent with four loving grandmothers, but the experience will be with them at a cellular level. I grew up surrounded by aunts and uncles and this weekend afforded them a similar experience of being enveloped by family love.

The two days in Portland were fruitful. We exhausted ourselves walking downtown Portland and adjacent neighborhoods. We even fit in a trip to visit the Columbia River Gorge. We enjoyed every minute of our trip: from Portland's scale to its famed network of public transit, its neighborhoods and parks, libraries, and restaurants. On the flight back to Oakland we discussed the pros and cons of relocating only to return again and again to the rich community of friends, acquaintances, and work colleagues we had built in Oakland. Our friends were our family. Some of them we had met decades earlier while we were college students. We knew their extended families and in some cases had traveled with them to visit their families in their respective countries. With our parents living in all corners of the United States and abroad—John's parents in Massachusetts and mine in Los Angeles and El Salvador—our community of friends were the backbone to our lives. Before the plane landed, we'd decided to remain in Oakland.

By February 2005, I was strong enough to revisit our original idea we'd had when we'd bought the house seven years earlier: to pour a new foundation and carry out a remodel of our existing house. Over restaurant meals I listened to John talk about what the new house could look like. Sometimes he drew sketches of our possible future house on napkins. Over messy Sunday pancake breakfasts, when struck with an idea, John would quickly reach for a pencil and sketch a house detail on a corner of newspaper. "We can do this," he'd say, and I'd see his architectural drawing skills unfolding in front of me. I inherited my papá's newspaper habit, which John also shares; our household has been, from the beginning, a two-newspaper home. Slowly, from napkin sketches to newspaper corner details, to more elaborate drawings on a sketch pad, I began to imagine a house that could meet our needs. Designing and overseeing the building of a new house, putting in all new systems, milling and installing interior carpentry, all on our own, with no general contractor, was a gargantuan undertaking. But that was the dream.

We reached out to an architect friend and shared our idea: reconfigure the existing house and build a second story to accommodate our family and have room for Mami in case she would like to join us. He was enthusiastic. On the spot, he agreed to make a preliminary set of drawings based on the sketches we gave him. Just like that, we opened a new door and let ourselves make new news. An agreement to remodel the house was an agreement to rewire myself. I did not know how things would unfold, but instinctively I knew that I was making the right call. Moving forward was like moving into a new country. I had to believe with all my might that this time the arrival would be home.

The house plans moved forward, I found a good rhythm with the kids at home, and a brand-new term started at the community college. One of the classes that called my attention was early in the morning. Edith agreed to babysit Izal on the days I had classes and John took Aurora to the preschool. All of my writing classes up to this point had been in the evening, so one day after class ended, I decided to poke around the Laney campus. Without thinking, I waltzed into the school's commons. I'd never been inside the building before. The space was abuzz with students sitting around tables, chatting, drinking coffee, eating breakfast. The cafeteria was located at the back of the space and the smell of breakfast foods hung thick in the atrium.

The cashier gave me a "You go, girl!" look when I stepped in front of her with my debit card in hand and a tray piled high with pancakes, scrambled eggs, and sausages. I'd walked into the cafeteria without any particular intention, and it was without thinking that I grabbed a tray, placed a white plate on it, and proceeded to order from the steaming platters. Everything called to me: the sausages, scrambled eggs, hash browns, even the pancakes, which, unless they were John's sublime buttermilk ones, I did not normally desire. I chose this and that and it all mounded on my plate. It took me longer to order the food than to eat it. When I stepped back out onto the quad and felt the fresh air on my face, I realized that that kind of boundless hunger could only mean one thing.

"Should we stop the construction project?" John asked when we left the doctor's office.

"No! Please, no," I said.

Nothing was going to dissuade me now from our remodel, not even a pregnancy. I had to move forward. I had to get on the other side of my fears.

We left the doctor's office where we'd seen our new baby floating inside the night of my womb. In two weeks, I would be through my first trimester, the doctor told us. To celebrate we headed to the nearest place we could think of—a local greasy spoon. The lunch-only venue was about to close but the cook let us order. It was a sunny midafternoon. We sat on the outdoor wooden picnic bench—the only seating available—and ordered hamburgers, fries, and vanilla shakes, the only items still available on the menu. We sat with our good fortune and ate heartily.

A few days later we drove to the city's planning department to pick up the approved permits for the house construction to begin. Either one of us could have gone on the errand alone. We knew the permits would be handed over a counter unceremoniously by a clerk, but we decided to go together like we had done when we submitted the offer to buy the house. We exited the building drunk with luck and love, with the confirmed news of our third child, with the approved permits to begin construction, stepping onto the threshold of a new phase in our lives.

The plan was to lift the existing structure twenty feet in the air and build an addition underneath. Our cottage was soon to be stripped of its roof, exterior siding, and interior plaster—everything but the wall studs—then lifted in the air and held in place with a hydraulic system. Then the exterior walls would be reconfigured to allow for windows and the interior walls reframed to make new room configurations. Our one-story, two-bedroom, one-bath house with a crumbling foundation and cottage cheese ceiling, was set to become a two-story, four-bedroom, three-bath house, with two offices and a covered porch in the backyard.

A neighbor around the corner had a duplex and his upstairs tenant had recently vacated. He agreed to rent us the apartment for the duration of our renovation. We packed and stored all but essential furnishings and kitchen items. I filled our red wheelbarrow with dishes, pots, and pans and, with my growing belly leading the way, moved our kitchen into the apartment around the corner. It took the construction crew two days to strip the house of its exterior siding, to tear out windows, doors, and interior plaster. In a mere forty-eight hours the house was reduced to a shell, leaving exposed the original 1906 redwood studs. In a week the entire house was up on hydraulic cribbing. The front garden was trampled into oblivion; the demo machinery simply careened over the sages, pinks, and roses. The plans called for the new house to move two feet forward, toward the street and into the front garden. The construction crew didn't know that my papá had planted the flowering David Austin roses.

John handled all the construction details. After we put the kids to bed, he pored over drawings, priced out materials, scheduled payments. Every night after 10 P.M., he grabbed the powerful flashlight he'd bought and walked around the corner to inspect the construction site. A ladder was stolen from the site the first week of construction. John said we had too many subcontractors leaving materials on site, and we needed to make sure the house stayed safe. He hired a company to fence the perimeter of our property, rigged a lighting system that went on with a timer, and paid a security team to drive past the house several times during the night. Every morning before he left for his job, he walked around the corner to meet the crews that would work that day to insure everyone was on the same page.

One morning when Izal was particularly fussy, I took him around the neighborhood in the umbrella stroller to calm him down and incite a nap. What I saw on Dover Street took my breath away: The fencing in the front of the house was completely open, a massive cement truck parked in front of it, blocking traffic while it pumped concrete for the foundation and basement walls. Two green portable toilets sat in what had been the driveway. The subcontractor handling the cement and framing pored over plans and gave orders. The manufactured thunder of it all made my head spin. Across the street was our future, under construction. I helped John as much as I could, making decisions while holding down the home front. I took care of our two toddlers and managed my body, which, having twice before experienced the forty-week journey from conception to birth, knew the pilgrimage well.

The days rolled one into the next without much time to fear random folks on the street. Despite the construction management stress, this was a chance to recalibrate. Every new system overhaul in the Dover house echoed my own willing transformation fueled by the creativity of my nascent writing life and by the ultimate creative act unfolding in the universe of my womb. My new baby was developing safely, assuredly growing its own systems inside the warm, welcoming, secure house that was my body.

On the 16th of October at five in the morning, I woke up startled by a sharp pain splitting my lower back in half. It was time. The moon, immaculately round and translucent, hung from an uncompromised sky and watched over me as I moaned on my knees, clinging to the back seat of the minivan on our way to the hospital. Two hours later a glorious, almost-ten-pound baby boy wiggled on my belly.

With Luis, days old and nestled in a sling, I climbed a raw set of stairs to the freshly framed second floor of our new house to decide on the final layout for the main bathroom. All that remained of the old house, built by a widow displaced by the 1906 San Francisco fire, were a few redwood studs, their rich red hue contrasting with the blond of the new framing material. Soon they would be a memory covered by planes of sheetrock. But the essence and richness of the Bay Area forest from which they came would remain, informing the building and our own lives.

When the interior of the house was almost completed, we threw a backyard party to celebrate Luis's baptism. He was almost a year old. In a few weeks I would take our wheelbarrow with our kitchen belongings from the upstairs duplex to our new house. Four of us left the house and five of us returned to it. Next to the duplex lived a couple originally from Louisiana and now empty nesters. She had converted their garage into a small hair salon; he was a retired cop from the Oakland Police Department. She took a liking to me, and he enjoyed talking with John. They must have seen something of their younger selves in us. On our first full evening in our remodeled house, they appeared on our front door carrying two cardboard boxes with pots containing a full Creole dinner. "Welcome back," they said, and left us to our unpacking. We sat around the table with Luis in my arms, enjoying red beans and rice and a luscious sweet potato pie. Our neighbor's gesture was an affirmation of our decision to stay in the house and the best possible blessing to our new beginnings.

Tía Maura flew from Florida to attend Luis's baptism and become his godmother. Camila, Mami, and Tía Dalia came up from Los Angeles. My dear cousin Cecilia also drove up from Los Angeles with her son, James, who is a month older than Izal. Friends joined us, some coming from as far as Boston. We delighted in watching the children play with one another in the backyard. Camila played with Izal and James, who squealed at her antics. Baby Luis was passed from one set of loving arms to another and he, a good-natured baby, wiggled joyfully. It was a perfect sunny day, and we lingered outside under the protection of the tall pittosporums, which over the seven years we had owned the house, had become lush, tall sentinels covering the old, tired chain-link fence with their quaking leaves. The Santa Rosa plum laden with fruit that year was an easy target from which Mami and my tías plucked all the fruit they wanted.

Spanish and English entwined like a confluence of waters. Almost all of us spoke both languages fluently, or enough of one or the other; even the littlest ones swam unencumbered in the current. If my papá was still living in the United States, then he too would have been there, but it had been years since he'd returned to live in El Salvador. Abuela was there, up in the firmament. The fact that we had a baptism at all, which was the reason for our gathering, was the direct result of her influence on me. A sense of plenitude permeated the afternoon. There was no rainbow visible in the sky, though our elation and gratitude could easily have reflected one. Like old times back in El Salvador, we celebrated, family and friends, food and fête. Two generations of us celebrated. We were home. No one mentioned the war.

26

To Be a Champion

Atiquizaya, El Salvador, 1970 / Oakland, California, 2010

Everywhere, signs of the 1970 World Cup assaulted our senses. The image of Juanito, the tournament's mascot, and the white, green, and red stripes of the Mexican flag shaped into a "México 70" were hard to miss. Juanito showed up in the pages of the two newspapers Papá brought home every day. "México 70" appeared in posters advertising beer, was drawn on notebooks at school, and aired on television ads. In the weeks leading up to the World Cup, television and radio announcers said things like "¡La Copa se vive!" and asked, "How will you live la Copa?" The question was usually followed by a list of things you should have to live la Copa al máximo: television sets, refrigerators, cars. Some things we already had, like a television set. Others we didn't own, like a car.

I was moved by the excitement, even though I had a difficult time following the action. I only knew the most important part: When a team kicked the ball into their opponent's net, that was called gol; better said, that was called gooooooolllllllll!!!! This I also knew: El fútbol makes people happy and brings them together. For the weeks of la Copa, the country, Atiquizaya, Barrio el Ángel, my home, was in a good mood.

For the first time in history, El Salvador was to start as one of the sixteen teams in contention. "Es un honor estar en México," I heard people say over and over, and their chests lifted when they got to "honor." The enthusiasm was contagious. It even conquered Papá's otherwise serious and purposeful ways. Instead of spending time alone reading books, he was caught in the excitement, watching the games, visiting my uncle's house, keeping up with the scores, and even inviting folks to come watch the games in our living room. El Salvador's classifying group included Mexico. "They beat the shit out of us," Papà said at the end of the game: "Nos vergiaron, pero al menos allí estamos." *We live la Copa*, his smile told me. While having the national team playing in México was memorable, there was another equally exciting reason why that year's tournament was so big: Pelé, the world's best soccer player was taking part. Everyone cheered the national team, but more than anything, everyone cheered Pelé.

The tournament's final was between Brazil and Italy. Papá said the final game should be the best one yet and Pelé was going to be in it. In preparation for the game, he washed dozens of mangoes to take to Tío Pedro's house. He and his family lived next door to us in a house identical in shape, but without the beautiful courtyard and garden we had in ours. Papá washed each mango, carefully not wasting a drop of water because he had to haul our supply each night from the public fountain. He carried the water in a cántaro, a large, round pitcher, nestled between his shoulder and against his right ear as many times as needed until the various barrels we used for cooking, bathing, doing laundry, and washing dishes were full. Mami shouted from the corridor, "¡Roman, ya casi es mediodía!"—It is close to noon. Fluffy clouds shaped and reshaped themselves against a light-blue sky. Papá quickly dried the mangoes, put them in a basket, and headed next door. As he opened the shutters at the front of the house he noticed me right behind him, "¿Quéres venir?" he asked. I nodded. I did. I wanted to go with him. I looked at Mami, who held Camila in her arms. Her smile gave approval.

There were already many people in Tío Pedro's living room when we arrived. Tío Pedro was Abuela's brother and like a father to Papá, who became a teacher thanks in part to the guidance he received from Tío Pedro, who was a well-respected teacher himself. Many of the adults in the room were uncles or cousins, but my abuela and tías were not there. Neither was Mami. Fútbol was a thing for men and boys. I recognized some of the neighborhood boys who came to our house to watch television in the evenings. No other girls were present. The only light in the room came from the big television set that lived inside a commode. The two large windows that faced the street had been shuttered and the tall door that led to the courtyard was also closed.

The room was packed and the clapping that burst out when the championship game, Brazil versus Italy, started surprised me. Every time someone made a good play, or a foul was made against Italy many voices broke out at once:

"¡Que Bárbaro!"

"¡Que jugada!"

"¡Increíble!"

Then Tío Pedro settled everyone back down again. When someone from the Brazilian team scored, the room erupted into cheers and applause, everyone stood up at the same time, and whoever was in the next room came rushing in to catch the story and maybe a repeat of the action.

Halftime arrived. The mangoes in the basket were eaten. A few of the men went to the store to bring back beers. My father called me over to where he was sitting and absentmindedly put his arm around me. I was overjoyed. "Este juego es histórico. Hay que recordarlo," he said. People around us nodded enthusiastically in agreement. *I will remember this,* I told myself. All of it: the excitement in the room, the applause, the "aaaaay" when it got dangerous, the avocado-green of the soccer field on my uncle's color television, the blue world of the Brazilian flag, this arm around me, hugging me, keeping me close.

Papá asked me to go to our house and fetch more mangoes. I ran the five meters with my long hair flowing behind me like a cape. The aquas, oranges, and whites of the houses facing our street were bathed in light, the colors standing out against the hazy blue of the volcano hovering in the horizon. I knew that when I stepped into our courtyard, birds would be singing in the lush waves of our mango tree and iguanas would be basking, bobbing their heads over the sun-heated red tiles of our roof. After I returned, Brazil lifted the tournament's trophy. We, in turn, had mangoes, and joy.

*

I wrote the story above as I was completing an MFA in poetry at Mills College in Oakland. It received an honorable mention in the nonfiction category of that year's writing competition. My thirst for writing had taken me from Laney College in Oakland to Berkeley City College, which offered an Associates of Arts degree in Poetry, and eventually to Mills. I found the idea of an AA degree in Poetry exhilarating, and I aimed to complete it. But before I could, I applied to various colleges to obtain an MFA. Every school I applied to offered me admission, but I chose Mills. I did a round of phone calls to people I knew who had completed the same degree as mature students, and one woman who attended Mills told me that she felt like she was going to a spa every day she was on campus. I loved the analogy and fully understood what she meant when I became a student there. The Mills campus is small and stately, with beautifully tended gardens and open spaces.

Whereas my community college classes were composed of an eclectic blend of folks—students with their high school experience still fresh on their cheeks, retired folks pursuing a passion or writing hobby, and some like me in search of something—at Mills, students wrote technically accomplished poems and stories. I was the only parent in my graduating class, maybe the only one over thirty, and the one with the least experience as a writer. I was undeterred. I showed up in earnest and soaked up every experience my classmates and professors offered. I felt incredibly fortunate and every day on campus felt like I was at a spa for poets.

What drives a caterpillar to entomb itself in its cocoon, or a worm to ever deeper depths? To pluck the unsayable from a garden, to recover an atom of oneself, place it on a hand and unfurl it toward another as fern unfurls a frond, that is why I went back to those classes. Day after day, week after week.

27

The Heart Knows When

Oakland, California, 2007–2013

The ache followed me like a loyal dog. It was a determined pang. I learned to acknowledge it quietly by putting my right hand above my heart. "There, there, now," I'd say to myself. The gesture became second nature. Sometimes the pain faded in and out; at times it pierced my chest. I'd try to explain it to John: "It is like a dagger."

After my maternity leave ended, I went back to work full-time as an instructional coach supporting first year teachers. Izal and Aurora attended preschool, and I left Luis in Edith's care. One afternoon, after visiting a high school in the district notorious for its staffing shortages and instructional challenges, I sat at my desk and shared the day's difficulties with my cubicle colleague. The school was located on a busy arterial in a part of town known for police brutality, and economic disinvestment. I drove down this boulevard several times a week, past boarded-up buildings, past abandoned furniture on the side of the road, past the old man who sat on the concrete steps of a battered building staring straight ahead, watching cars swoosh by on their way to elsewhere.

Back at the office, Sarah, another colleague, pulled up a chair to join the conversation we had going in our cubicle and commented on my soothing action.

"What's going on there?" she asked leaning in my direction. "You keep on rubbing your arm and putting your hand over your chest."

"It's nothing," I said. "I get these chest pains sometimes. They come and go."

"Have you had your ticker checked lately?" Sarah asked. "It's not normal to have chest pain." She had grown up with an MD mother and took my gesture seriously. She called our boss over. Soon the entire office was insisting I go to the emergency room. I gave in to their persistence.

Once I was in the emergency room, staff moved fast. Before I knew it, I was wearing a yellow disposable gown. Vitals were taken, blood samples. My chest was dotted with electrodes hooked up to monitors. John awaited word in the austere waiting room where the only thing on the wall was a banner: "Heart attacks strike women differently. Learn to identify the symptoms." Several hours later I signed a release of liability stating that I was leaving against doctor's orders and at my own risk. It was after 10 P.M. when I stepped through the front door of our house. John had left the hospital earlier to take care of the children and was up, sitting in the living room, waiting for me. He had fed, bathed, and put all three to bed. After hours of observation in a hospital bed, dressed in yellow paper garb, a battery of tests yielded no answers. I knew I was not having, nor had I ever had, a heart attack.

Unfortunately, that was not the only time I checked in to a hospital with heart attack symptoms. Many years later, living in a different city, writing about El Salvador had long ceased to be about pleasant memories. The second time I was hospitalized I'd spent the morning writing about my cousin Lauro's killing. Later in the day, helped by John, I was on my way to the emergency room, experiencing shortness of breath and acute pain as if my heart were being stabbed. It made no difference to my body that Lauro's tragic death was decades in the past. I felt the loss, and all the losses surrounding his death, as keenly as the day my papá walked into the house back in San Salvador with the grim news. I was much older now, living in different country, in a house big enough to seek solace in a garden, but the memory nevertheless controlled my body, made it relive the terror and feel the freefall into grief. Bone and sinew, muscle and membrane could not distinguish between yesteryear and the now.

Years after my first visit to the emergency room at Alta Bates Summit Medical Center in Berkeley, I was again hooked up to machines that linked up to monitors that displayed the activity of a normal heart. No machine or medical test, as sophisticated as they were, detected any aberrations or the ache lodged inside my chest cavity. The heartache I felt that day was physically real and also emotional. Both discernable to only the eye that knows everything.

Unlike Alta Bates, where John was made to sit in the waiting room, this hospital allowed him into the observation room with me. With John by my side, I retraced my doings in the early part of the day. I didn't shout "eureka," but I could have. I could have run out onto the street wearing the flimsy paper hospital garb and shouted to the world that I'd just come to grips with the non-fairy-tale tale ending of my family's escape from war. When we left El Salvador, we thought we were leaving the war behind, but we brought it with us! It lives in our bodies! War lives in my heart, under my eyelids, lurking in watershed of my nervous system. It takes shelter in my hands, which in turn, peel, fray, and tremble. Decades after the peace treaty was signed and the war officially relegated to history books, a patient was still being brought to an emergency room with war wounds. It seemed incongruous, even ridiculous. I laughed. John laughed with me. I don't suffer from heart disease. I live with war. That is my medical condition.

What my parents could not have known that January 17 morning when we stepped on United States soil for the first time is that they rescued us from war only to live in a country where a low-grade war rages rampant every day. Thousands of people in the United States die from gun violence every year. Thousands more rot in jail. Even more die unsheltered, or from untreated illnesses. Meanwhile, racism whittles away at people's bodies and spirits, in some cases facilitating the onset of other health conditions. My family escaped state violence in one country to endure other forms of violence in the new country. My first visit to the hospital when I worked in Oakland was the result of my daily interactions with students who lived in veritable minefields, dealing with guns and drugs, poverty, racism, death. The second time was the result of delving deeply into my memories of our life in El Salvador during the war. To my body the linguistic and geographical differences were immaterial. Violence is violence.

Walking / Caminando

Walking

Caminando

Walking

Caminando

Walking

Caminando

Walking

Soon after moving back into our remodeled house, I took the children to play a block away in the brand-new park built in our neighborhood. For years the field behind the old Merritt College had been an abandoned, weed-infested, chain-linked lot. The children's hospital a couple of blocks away bought the building under the promise that it would respect the exterior architectural features of the college while converting the interior of the building into a hospital research facility on one side and a community senior center on the other. Under the plan, the weed-infested lot was to become a city park.

The children's hospital refurbished the college as stated. The senior center became a reality, and the indoor gym was transformed into a community meeting space. It took much longer for the rectangle-shaped space at the rear of the building to become a park. But when it did, it was planted on the perimeter with a variety of grasses and yellow roses and featured a generous field and a children's playground with purple climbing and sliding equipment. My children came to call it Purple Park. One day while the children played, I picked up a conversation with another parent who told me that a family who had recently moved into the neighborhood had been harassed and accosted by a group of older kids. The subtext was that the older kids were Black and up to no good. As I heard the story an internal fire seized me and in a second two things became crystal clear:

1. I was not going to abide the park becoming the province of a few, to the point where families with young children or school-aged children on their own would be scared to use it.
2. I would not entertain the argument that Black teenagers in the neighborhood were troublemakers. It is too easy to blame others, especially young people, for one's own discomfort and fears. I knew too well that it is a slippery slope to make assumptions about people.

Papá was once handcuffed and thrown into the back seat of a police car. He had been waiting to catch a bus in El Monte, California, where we lived. The police held him without informing him why he was arrested. When the police let him go, they told him the red shirt he was wearing fit the description of a suspect. Papá came home shaken to the core, looking like he had seen a ghost. We knew racial profiling, more than the shirt, was the reason for his detainment. Papá's experience often ran through my mind for those weeks after the shooting when I walked around, a ghost myself, irrationally afraid. Like my papá, I have had experiences where my intentions and integrity have been doubted because of the way I look. It was clear to me that the solution to the violence described by my neighbors was not to stop using the park, but to use it more.

All of us in the neighborhood had the right to use the park safely: those of us with young families, the seniors in our neighborhood, the afterschool kids, the older teenagers, the weed smokers, the early-morning tai chi lady, the goat owners down the street who brought their animals for an early morning graze on the lawn. If I wanted to live in a peaceful neighborhood, then I had to do my part to create it.

The days of the weed-infested lot were not so far back as to have been easily forgotten. Those of us who had been in the neighborhood long enough knew how depressing the alternative to the park we now had looked like. I talked to Mr. V., one of our venerable neighborhood stewards, who happened to live on Aileen two houses down from where the shooting had taken place. Would he support me, I asked, if I convened monthly Sunday meetings at the park? This would give neighbors a chance to meet or catch up with one another and at the same time pick up trash around the park, pull a few weeds here and there, put in the effort for our local public space. What if we all brought a treat to share and made it an outdoor gathering? Sure, Mr. V. said, he would support me. John also thought it was a good idea.

I made flyers and a few days later leafleted the neighborhood. I called the gatherings First Sunday of the Month at Dover Park. I left flyers under doormats, in mailboxes, rolled up in door handles. I talked to anyone who would engage with me, walking up to their homes or sitting on a porch. I put my energy and conviction into my exchanges with people. Back in Atiquizaya, I had seen my parents attend meetings and talk with strangers to inspire them about possibilities for change. Dover Park was not El Salvador. But it activated what I had learned from my parents about civic involvement.

The first Sunday meeting was a resounding success. Adults, children, seniors, babies, neighbors bearing muffins, coffee cakes, deviled eggs, and other snacks showed up. Peter, our neighbor around the corner, showed up with his guitar and played while the rest of us got to know one another. The local council representative sent one of her aides to say that she endorsed our effort at community building. At one point during the two hours the gathering lasted, I stood up on a picnic table, thanked everyone for attending, and explained the purpose of the gathering. Folks wrote their email on the sign-in sheet I'd brought along. I walked away from the park that morning with a working list of Dover Park supporters.

Whenever John tells this story he lingers on the part when I stood on the picnic table. I did it spontaneously when I noticed my height was preventing me from addressing the entire crowd. When we returned to the house, John told me that I'd made a great presentation and appeal for neighbors to become involved in the stewardship of the park. He also teased me that at that instant I'd become the mayor of Dover Park. He called me that from then on.

Some first Sundays had excellent turnouts and sometimes only a handful of people showed up. There was the year the first Sunday landed on January first. At ten in the morning, I was the only one there; everyone else was doing what people do on New Year's Day. Alone and undeterred, I went to work, assigning myself the task of deadheading the rose bushes and picking up trash.

The city of Oakland ran a park stewardship program. I signed up and became an official park steward for the city and chose Dover Park as my responsibility. There were four of us who were the core group. We met in one another's backyards to plan and strategize on behalf of the park. In the fall, we planted dozens of daffodil bulbs provided by the city. Each spring we organized a massive cleanup and beautifying effort on Earth Day. Each fall we celebrated neighborhood night out on the park grounds. I routinely sent upbeat emails to my Dover Park working group as the first Sunday approached to get people out to the park. I set up a blog and swept the park's perimeter for trash every time I brought my kids and encouraged others to do the same. Over time litter declined. When graffiti appeared on the back wooden fence, a neighbor half a block away took it upon himself to quickly paint over it with the best matching green paint he could find. A husband-and-wife team who were professional gardeners planted sages and other drought-tolerant perennials left over from one of their projects. Ever so slowly, my dream that we, collectively, would take on the care of the park by using it, sharing it, welcoming everyone, and keeping it clean was unfolding.

Mr. V. and I attended a community meeting at the senior center regarding cutbacks to the city's park budget. As the meeting ended, the council aide who knew of our efforts at Dover Park introduced us to a young pediatrician and a young man who had recently started a food justice nonprofit. They asked us if we would we be interested in setting up a community garden at Dover Park. Mr. V. and I looked at each other. Was this a joke? The offer was too good to be true. The doctor and the food activist commanded an impressive group of eager volunteers. Now in addition to First Sundays we had Weekly Wednesdays. We chose the north-side entrance to the park to start our vegetable beds. We decided against enclosures around the vegetable garden. Any fruits of our labor could be harvested by anyone. The garden belonged to us all and would remain accessible for those who needed it most. Together, we swept up the neighborhood into a swirl of civic work and pride. I wrote a grant to build raised beds for seniors and wheelchair-bound gardeners. The doctor worked with obese children at the children's hospital, and she routinely brought some of her young patients to the park to learn about gardening and about how food is grown. Even cooking demonstrations were part of these events.

The local school children made whimsical wooden signs depicting pollinators and staked them in our vegetable beds. Summer arrived and, with the collaboration of one of the neighbors next to the park, we hung a white sheet from two long posts and projected movies under the stars. One August for Night Out we rolled our barbecues to the park grounds and cooked a prodigious number of hot dogs. No one vandalized the garden, no one trampled it, no one uprooted the plants, nor harvested all the produce at once. On volunteering days, we each walked away with peppers, zucchinis, corn, kale—the fruits of our labor were collectively harvested.

At that point, I was enrolled in poetry classes at Berkeley Community College. After class one day, a classmate asked me if I would like to join his writing group. James had published his poems in local and national journals. The poems he read in class told me he had been very active during the Sanctuary movement in the 1980s, even getting arrested for his opposition to the United States' involvement in El Salvador. It touched me deeply that, after all the years, someone who had understood the injustices of the US intervention in El Salvador and risked his skin to oppose them was now asking me to be part of his writing community. The group met once a month and we rotated though our homes to hold our workshops. Nancy lived in a Berkeley senior housing building and when we met at her cheerful studio, we sat on her bed and on every available corner we could find.

Farmworkers Day was on the horizon and the volunteers at the park asked me to emcee Dover Park's first Day of Service. I accepted, and in turn asked James and two other poets from the Berkeley class to share the stage with me. The Day of Service included a poetry reading, a health fair, and a garden workday. The local television station even showed up to cover it. The First Sunday of the Month was now an established routine in the neighborhood. What had started as my effort to cultivate peace and community building was now bigger, and included bringing awareness to issues of food justice, child obesity, and land stewardship.

I learned to hold the tug of my emotions whenever I went by the corner of Aileen and Dover Streets. There had been a time when my entire body winced approaching the intersection by foot or on wheels. One Sunday after a garden workday I discovered something had shifted inside me. With Aurora and Izal walking next to me, I dragged the red wagon filled with garden tools, water jugs, and a tired Luis, who'd sneaked into the wagon. I stood on the curb across the Dover and Aileen street signs and realized these streets intersected the events of June 19, 2003, memories of the civil war, and the very moment I was living—a moment charged with joy and grounded in community.

When I acquiesced to the house's remodel, I was fully aware that my decision to stay in the neighborhood also meant that I would be living in proximity to a source of trauma. Walking home tired from a morning of community gardening and park cleanup, taking happy, hungry children home to lunch, was more than a triumph. I forged a new reality for myself every Sunday we volunteered at the park. I was contributing to the kind of community to which I wanted to belong, while at the same time acknowledging the events that shaped my life in Oakland and in El Salvador. I held in my hands my piece of the puzzle that tells my family's history of exile and arrival.

One Sunday, as we prepared to head to the park for a workday, Aurora decided to make and sell lemonade. When we bought the house we inherited a Meyer lemon and a Santa Rosa plum. Engulfed in rampant grass, the lemon was hardly a tree all those years ago. Over the time, with proper care, it became a strong, prolific yielder of prized lemons.

Standing at the kitchen counter on their stools, Aurora, Izal, and Luis squeezed sunshine from the morning's harvest and made pitchers of lemonade with my help. We secured the pitchers and an array of colorful plastic cups in the red wagon. Aurora made a sign: "Lemonade 5 cents." I asked her if she would like to charge a little more per glass, twenty-five cents maybe? No, she said, everyone could afford a glass at five cents. At the park, my children set up pitchers, cups, and the sign on one of the park's picnic tables. One of the gardeners handed Aurora a dollar bill and invited everyone volunteering to come have a glass. The children beamed, touching us with their starlight's glow.

28

Alphabets

West Palm Beach, Florida, 1981

A black-and-white photo accompanies an article inside the January 30, 1981, edition of the *Evening Times* profiling my family's arrival in the US. You may see it in gray tones, but I see it flushed in color, as if we had posed for it yesterday. We had been in the US thirteenth days when the photograph was taken. On January 17 Tía Maura picked us up at Miami Airport. The four of us were exhausted and exhilarated from our trip's ordeal. We had escaped the war and arrived safely, but we had left so much behind. Each of us carried a small suitcase. Papá managed his, plus a cardboard box filled with books he'd selected to make the trip with us. We packed ourselves into Tía Maura's sedan and rolled north toward West Palm Beach, where Aunt Maura had rented us a house. The house was plain and white and sat on the corner of a fenceless lot. The sedan made its way to the end of the block and the white house appeared to me like a white handkerchief held high in a combat zone, a gesture of surrender and peace.

In contrast to the four of us, reeling still from the sound of ricocheting bullets and spinning helicopter rotor blades, the reporter from the *Evening Herald* appeared cheerful and optimistic. She asked questions, mostly directed at my parents, while Camila and I sat quietly nearby. After the interview, the photographer from the *Herald* arranged us in the middle of the living room and, with a blinding flash, captured what the four of us wore on our faces that day. In the photograph, Mami, elegant as ever, sits triumphantly in a black suit and an emerald-green silk blouse. She was the architect of our escape: It was her efforts and Tía Maura's dogged, single-minded vision that allowed this moment to take place.

Papá wore a gray sweater over a fine-checkered red-and-blue button-down shirt, his pose that of an affable patriarch. His hand rests protectively on my shoulder, in a gentle gesture. Camila and I wore the outfits we put on the day we left El Salvador. With her head tilted and her lips curling into a shy smile, Camila is the child who remains under the security of her parents. The scalloped edge of her cream sweater underscores her innocence. Everyone looks directly at the camera, and everyone manages a smile, except me. I look mistrustful and awkward, my hands bent at the wrists and folded into shadow fists. The inward curling of my hands responded to all that we had given up to be in that sunny living room.

When we first arrived in the US, we all experienced symptoms of war trauma. My father slept poorly and suffered from dreams of persecution. Any sudden noise or movement made us anxious and startled. Our bodies tensed up at the sight of anyone in a police uniform. The memory of uniformed soldiers and police back in El Salvador shadowed our existence. Yet slowly, perhaps predictably, the war's tentacles eased their choke on us.

The new experiences, foods, and sights we encountered in the US helped to distract us—at least immediately after our arrival—from the war we left behind. For Camila and me, the fact that thick chocolate milk was available 24/7 on supermarket shelves was a bit of sparkling magic. My first pineapple sundae from Dairy Queen lives on in my body as gustatory glory. My first fast-food burger not so much. Tía Maura had stocked the refrigerator with novel foods, like that first half gallon of chocolate milk. She made us peanut butter sandwiches with a jar that swirled grape jelly with peanut butter. They met with our approval. For a few years every experience was a new one: new jobs, new schools, new grades, pick-your-own grapefruits and berries, Halloween night and pumpkin patches, outdoor barbecues, Thanksgiving celebrations.

We learned a new language and adopted new customs. Years went on, and by virtue of human adaptability I began to believe these customs had always been our own, and not only ours, but that of our parents and our grandparents, knowing perfectly well that it is an impossibility, knowing it's something we don't wish for at all, but the allegiance to the new place grows strong enough to let the illusion slide.

Living in the United States for five years as green-card holders made us eligible to apply for American citizenship. We let decades go by before any one of us chose to do so. Even after it became clear to me that I had made a life in the US, decades after I started dreaming in English, writing in English, many years after I learned this country's history and lore, I refrained from seeking citizenship. The reality of the US involvement in the war that killed thousands, that provoked my family and thousands of my compatriots to flee, and continue to flee, remained raw and painful. This fact has not changed. But not being able to vote in elections and the birth of my children made me finally accept that my life is here in the United States. Members of my extended family who have emigrated are, like me, ensconced in private, professional, civic, religious, educational, artistic, and sports communities. We live in the US and are part of the Salvadoran diaspora.

I set a beautiful table at Thanksgiving, as does every member of my family who lives in the US. We swoon over homemade pumpkin and pecan pies. Each February on Super Bowl Sunday, we gorge on guacamole, hoot at the extravagant TV commercials, and root for our respective favored teams. I do this even when the rules of the game, after over forty years of living in the US, remain as unclear to me as the morning after a particularly loud college party. Yes, my actions say, I am from here, I belong here. This is my home.

I anticipate summer days and mark the season's big holiday: the Fourth of July. Over the years I've been part of lovely gatherings and outdoor events where people I've just met suddenly feel like longtime friends. I might like the peach cobbler, or a plate of BBQ and corn off the grill, or baked beans and coleslaw, but the reason I celebrate Fourth of July is my appreciation of how it invites community. Yet the patriotic posturing and jingoistic bent that can also be part of the day leaves a bitter taste, a sharp reminder of the violences, destructions, and displacements that US foreign policy has wrought in countries like El Salvador.

Life in the US is a set of contradictions. There is no space large enough in any book to hold the gratitude I feel for my parents' bravery in making the difficult choice to leave El Salvador and bring Camila and me to a place that held the promise of a tomorrow. The biggest opportunity the United States has given us is the chance to live, to rest at night, barring illness, knowing that in all probability we will wake up to a fresh new day, knowing that this simple but amazing act may be repeated day after day, year after year. Yet, in my lifetime I've also experienced the dark side of the United States: I know that housing and employment discrimination exist. I know that racism is real and that it pollutes every aspect of society. I know the sting of low expectations sometimes placed on students of color. Plenty of times I've smelled the sourness emitting from folks before experiencing their disregard of my personhood.

Our first years in the US were difficult. After living in Florida for six months, my parents decided to move to New Jersey with the help of another one of Mami's sisters who had emigrated with Tía Maura in the late sixties. Lodi, New Jersey proved too cold for us, and so my parents, at the invitation of my papà's sister who lived in California, moved us to the Greater LA area. I completed eleventh and twelfth grade in El Monte. Midway through my senior year, as students were preparing college applications, my counselor brought me into her office. She told me in her cramped office that she did not think I was college material. My SAT scores were very low, she said. I knew that already. I sat for the tests only a few days after coming down with chickenpox. My parents had paid for my exam fee. I had to show up. I arrived at the testing facility feeling poorly from a fever. I struggled through the exams—except for the Spanish exam, in which I excelled. I had been in the US for two and half years and my English-language skills were not yet there. It takes about seven years to master a language, I later learned. Given my scores, the counselor suggested I complete two years of community college before seeking a transfer to a four-year school. I understood this to be a fine strategy, but it was not what I wanted to do, nor was it the dream I'd worked for. My abuela's feistiness ran deep in me. I trusted my intuition and walked out of the meeting determined to move forward with my plan. Each of my college applications, done completely on my own, went to four-year universities.

My school held a senior assembly every year to acknowledge the graduating class. The entire school gathered in the gym; the seniors sat on chairs arranged on the gym's floor and everyone else was arranged by grade level on the bleachers. Awards were given for each of the main academic disciplines, for ASB service, and for athletic performance. The school administration read the names of students and the universities to which they had been accepted. We clapped and cheered and hollered as each name was called. The English award went to me. They called my name and announced at the same time that the University of California, Irvine had accepted me. The award was completely unexpected. No doubt I was a dedicated student, but I struggled mightily. I toiled over reading and writing assignments, but found time to report for the school newspaper and was part of the team that published our literary magazine. The English faculty who made the award choice were saying: "We see you, Claudia, we believe in you."

Our first full year in the US was 1982. Life was safe compared to El Salvador, but also small. We were one another's only reference points in the absence of our large extended family and my parents' network of friends and work colleagues. Our world dulled in contrast to the tropical sun that suffused everything in El Salvador. Concerns were of a different kind: finding jobs and schools, learning English. My parents struggled to make ends meet. Mami cleaned houses and worked an assembly line checking transistor parts. In West Palm Beach Papá had washed dishes at a seafood restaurant, in New Jersey he cleaned a factory's floors, in LA he mowed lawns. My parents struggled with their marriage. They struggled to afford the comfort they did give us, just as their hearts tried to find warmth beneath all the wounds.

Little by little, Camila and I swapped Spanish for English, at first practicing single words with each other.

"Battery," I said in my thick accent.

"Battery," she repeated in her nascent American one.

School, *The Brady Bunch*, *Happy Days*, and other TV shows propelled us into fluency. We went from words to phrases to sentences and the day arrived when Spanish was no longer necessary—or wanted—between us. With a university degree in English from El Salvador, Mami's English became more fluent every day. Papá struggled. Washing dishes and doing janitorial work required minimal English fluency. The English he acquired as a university student was for reading texts, not for maneuvering through the challenges he faced every day. He spiraled downward—the less able he was to communicate in English, the worse he felt about himself, and the bigger the gap between him and Mami became. English filled our world the way a cotton ball inside a glass tube absorbs water. There was less and less space left for Papá inside our tubes. With time, our Spanish began to collect dust. Eventually, perhaps inevitably, the Spanish words that may have helped us make sense of our experience and our exile became messages inside glass bottles adrift at sea.

I spoke Spanish at home and only to my parents. Camila and I practiced English with each other so much it became our de facto language. From the first days of our arrival, I focused so intently on acquiring English that my effort had eroded my Spanish as a result. In college I met two brothers from Honduras, Silas and Alex, who had also arrived in the US as teenagers like me. One of them became my boyfriend; the other, a lifelong friend. They were avid readers and worked just as avidly to maintain their Spanish. They read in Spanish. They told me about the shows they attended, including readings in Spanish. They also wrote poetry in Spanish and even put together a small chapbook, which I still own to this day. "Who are you?" they seemed to ask whenever I stumbled, trying to make a point in my halting Spanish. They teased me relentlessly. What they were saying was: "Claudia, don't forget yourself. Don't forget yourself."

Sitting on the sand in the shadow of the Newport Beach pier on my first date with Silas, we had a meandering conversation and talked about our Central American childhoods. He also mentioned writers he loved and rhapsodized about Gabriel García Márquez in particular. I was eighteen years old; I'd never heard of García Márquez. On a weekend visit to my parents' place, I found *Cien años de soledad* among Papá's books. I read it in gulps, mesmerized and transfixed. I marveled, I laughed, I cried, I saw myself. Márquez's Macondo was like my Atiquizaya: thrumming with life and color, full of epic stories and small stories, stories of the living, of the dead, and of the spirits that bridge worlds. The characters that populated Macondo were like my living relatives, like my beloved abuela. The book cast my life in Atiquizaya in an entirely different light: We were flawed, yes, and also beautiful.

This awareness slipped slowly into me. My relatives and I were not adrift in the morass of the colonial narrative we had been taught at school; we had agency. There were forces—political, economic, historical—that pushed against us, but we pushed back. We shaped ourselves too. Our very existence was a testament to resistance and resilience, to faith and love. Those stories I wrote in my early writing efforts at Laney College in Oakland owe something to this time in my life. The awakening I experienced with my Honduran friends was the beginning of the return to myself.

When I live inside the Spanish language my personal boundaries dissolve. My self is diluted in language. I am the language. Spanish works on me like a secret code. It unlocks every cell in my body. It makes everything rush into me: air, sun, elation, fear, insults, joy. In English I construct houses. Everyday a new one. Imperfections in usage do not bother me. They remind me that I live in territory that requires alertness and invites discovery. My errors in usage say that part of me belongs elsewhere. That elsewhere is a green rainbow; the heart of the mother tree moors there, generous and lush with birdsong.

English is neither ahead nor behind me. It keeps its distance. When I live in English, I take a break from the patriarchy embedded in the Spanish language. In Spanish if there are ten sisters present, the noun is "hermanas," but the moment a brother enters the picture, the noun switches to the masculine, "hermanos." There could be one hundred sisters and one brother, and the noun would still be "hermanos." My children may not know the person I am in my Spanish country, but they will know the person who chose to construct a new home, who chose to live closer to her truth every day. It is a choice. Spanish is a belonging. English, a freedom. They are not mutually exclusive. And they both belong to me.

*

"El Salvador: America Offers One Family a Chance to Forget Fears." That is the title from the *Evening Times* article. That is how Mary Ann, the reporter, or her editor, labeled our experience. The word "forget" jumps out at me every time I read it, which is often, as the newspaper page featuring the article has been, for years, framed and displayed in a corner of my living room. Forgetting is what my family for decades worked hard to do. All of us worked hard not to look back at the things that forced our exile. We worked not to linger too long when we recalled the extended family we left behind; we worked to brush aside pangs of longing for El Salvador. We were busy moving forward, learning English, carving our way through the wood of our new country. "Don't look behind," we were told. "Look forward, this is your chance at the American Dream!" Without fully knowing what that meant, we forged ahead. Onward.

Decades passed before any of us had time to think about what it means to belong fully to a place in such a way as to be indistinguishable from its language, the way we were in El Salvador. To dissolve into the vernacular, into language and landscape, like ingredients in bread, one indistinguishable from the other, is a kind of luxury. It has taken me years to understand that to move forward we first needed to look back. To arrive at this moment, scratching letters into a notebook at 10:50 P.M. on a Tuesday night, I needed to retrace the steps my family took forty years ago. I make words on paper out of necessity. At first, I could not see my life's words clearly. I skulked around the chiaroscuro of their charge. These words here came from far away, traveling the distance of years, the distance of miles; they traveled the distance of memory. One word in front of another yielded poems, sometimes sentences, often light. One word in front of the other paved a road, then another. One day I realized I had a map, a map of my geography. I assure you, the writing in these pages is that map.

29

Libros

Oakland, California, 2008

The day we left El Salvador we carried with us four small suitcases and a box of books. I've lived with, and lugged, these books, with titles such as *Nuestro Idioma*, *Historia de El Salvador*, *El Materialismo Histórico*, for decades. I have carried them from West Palm Beach in Florida to Los Angeles, to Europe, where I lived in my mid-twenties, back to Los Angeles, then to Oakland. All those years waiting for the right time to read them, waiting for the moment when I'd need them. At low points, especially during my many moves, I've wanted nothing more than to get rid of these books.

The fact was that decades after leaving El Salvador, these yellowing volumes filled with academic Spanish, mathematical formulas, treatises on historical materialism, these books still held an irreversible spell on me. One summer, in the newly renovated house, I came very close to getting rid of them. Armed with determination, I unfolded the aluminum ladder to the attic and climbed into its sweltering heat. My idea was to rip off the title covers and haul the rest of the pages down to the recycling bin. I took the first book out of the box and tore off the cover, but regret settled immediately in the space where the cover had been. The plan failed, same as my previous attempts.

The books in Papá's library back in El Salvador met three types of fate. The first was to escape the country with their spines intact. These were the books in my attic. The second fate was to be lost, scattered here and there with friends and relatives—I lost my own childhood book collection this way. The third group of books suffered the worst fate. Those are the books that are most likely still buried in the backyard of the last house we inhabited in El Salvador. In the final days before we left for the US, Papá exhumed the boxes he'd hidden under the stairs of the house on Pasaje Jupiter in Colonia Satélite and reburied them in the backyard. He buried them close to the fence, where the wild mangoes grew, and the mockingbirds sang their songs.

I don't know what went through my papá's head on those wrenching last days in El Salvador. What made him decide to pack the books we brought? Or given the danger, why decide to pack books at all? A man of few words, he has never spoken about his choice, letting his actions speak for themselves. One thing is certain: The books waited decades, in dark spaces and dank corners, for me to unlock the riddle of their presence among my belongings.

When I opened the box, that afternoon in the attic, and saw their familiar backs, the lettering on their covers, my determination withered. I was only able to tear the cover from a single book. I knew these books well. Like distant relatives, they were family. These books knew me as Claudia in El Salvador and they know me now as Claudia in the United States. The girl I was and the woman I have become.

In the sweltering heat, I came to terms with the fact that I'm never going to need any of the books. I'm never going to read *Matemáticas modernas*, or peruse *Historia social de la ciencia* on a lazy afternoon. I finally understood that I couldn't get rid of them because doing so would mean betraying Papá and giving away a part of myself. The books are physical proof that there once was an alternate route to my life, a route that did not include the gash of exile. They are a bridge to a possible self that will never be. They are a poem and witnesses of my papá's love.

My family's immigration story, like so many others before us, is a story of grit, gratitude, sacrifice and perseverance. We gained a new home in the US, and we lost one in El Salvador. Both things are true. The books remind me that it is possible to experience gain and loss in the same breath. Our successes do not diminish the suffering and the loss of having left everything we owned, what we knew, everything and everyone we held dear in El Salvador.

In fact, experiencing the loss, understanding what the war took from us, is precisely what magnifies our gain. The terror we endured and the struggles we overcame are exactly what gives our life in the United States its radiance and plenitude. I realized that the books knew both sides of my family's experience: the full lives we had before the war and the toils we went through upon our arrival in this country. At that moment up in the attic, I understood ourselves not as immigrants, but as people with wide horizons, capable of conjuring the contours and contents of two worlds, two languages, two ways of being.

I was not alone in that attic. The intervening spirit that saved my life—and those of my children the day of the shooting—was present. Also present was the spirit that looked over me my years in college and graduate school. My abuela was there too, as she has been from the day I came into the world. My heart overflowed with gratitude for the sacrifices my parents made for me and my sister and for all the people, friends, teachers, and strangers who've helped me along the way.

Some people are more porous than others. I belong with those in the more permeable ranks. The things I lived and witnessed in El Salvador lodged themselves deeply into gristle and bone and I carried a deep sorrow with me for a long, long, time. Unaware of it, my life grew around it. It and I became one. The war trauma and the difficulties of immigration, the relentless drone of racism, sexism, and the elitism of academia only deepened my sorrow. I felt ugly and diminished. In those dim places I was someone defined as lacking something, no matter what, when, or how I did things. For years I treaded water and floundered against the pull of this negative undertow. I felt lost. I longed for myself.

The bullets fired the day of the shooting defiled my house and my body. My body and the house, shards and dust. The bullets also shattered my way of being in the world. It took decades, but out of the wreckage, and after years of writing, my sorrow has finally lessened. Out of the rubble, a new house to hold my own growing family surfaced. Out of the ashes, I emerged with a clear understanding of the history and people to whom I belong. I am a war survivor. I am meant to be a writer. This is part of what I realized in the sweltering attic. Without being aware of Abuela's north star, her determination and strength helped me stay afloat, helped me not succumb to bleak narratives, to my sadness, anxiety, and fears. Writing is a gift bestowed on me. This gift has been the medium that has allowed me to get on the other side of myself. Word by word, with pen in hand, I am both the main character and narrator of my own life. The grief has not left me; it is still there. Because of it I have become a more expansive person.

On my first visit to El Salvador, eleven years after our exile, I saw with clear eyes the country's lushness and beauty. El Salvador is a ball of tangled greens: parrot greens curl around emerald greens and flowers, like precious gems, sparkle and emanate hues charged with sunlight. In that homecoming, sipping coffee with family in the house I'd grown up in, doves cooed from the branches of the large and unruly fruit trees. The cooing told of peace, as if the war had never happened. Birds sang before, during, and after the war. Birdsong at sunrise, birdsong at sundown, songs of living, a perennial heartbeat drum. El Salvador's birds sang their throaty tunes and her flowers bloomed during the terror years and met us on the other side full of color and music.

In fact, El Salvador's terrain, flora, fauna, and the magic and fire of her volcanoes, have been there, inspiring, instilling resilience and joy in her people since time immemorial. To view El Salvador and its people only as a forlorn place corroded by poverty, violence, and repression is to only see half the picture. It has taken me decades to fully metabolize this understanding. I hold it now as I have made more room for music, for birdsong, and for the maraca leaf-rustling of trees inside myself.

30

Faith

El Monte to Oakland, California, 2008

My parents divorced in the early 1990s. The stress of the war years, the adjustments to life in the US, and their own personal struggles forced their decision. By 1995, Mami remarried and moved to Costa Rica with her new husband. Camila was out of college and living on her own in Orange County, California. Tía Gina had also divorced her husband and Papá moved in with her, her two boys, Junior and Alfredo, and Abuela. I had been living in Europe and when I put an end to my longtime, serious relationship, I asked Papá if I could move in with him. He was still working as a gardener in the Greater LA area. Tía worked long days at her two Salvadoran restaurants. Abuela stayed home making meals, taking my youngest cousin to school. They still lived in El Monte, in a three-bedroom house with a clipped lawn and short rose bushes planted along a low white fence. Tía slept in the main room, Abuela shared a room with Junior while, Alfredo, who was then in high school, turned the garage into his den. Papá shared his room with me while I searched for a teaching job and got back on my feet. We shared his queen bed and, since we had similar habits, fell into a routine quickly: We went to bed with a book and when we were both satisfied with our respective reading we turned off our bedside light, turned our backs to each other, and fell asleep.

I applied for an emergency teaching credential, enrolled in Cal State Los Angeles's teachers program, and soon found a full-time position as a first-grade bilingual teacher in an elementary school in nearby Pasadena. On days when I did not have credential classes I came home after school just in time to watch Univision's early evening news with Abuela. The news was preceded by the great and very flamboyant Puerto Rican diviner, Walter Mercado. Abuela and I hung on to every word of Walter's daily horoscopes and exhaled only when he arrived at his signature closing phrase: "Les deseo mucho, mucho AMOR." Then came the evening news and two more telenovelas. My abuela, my tía, and Papá never asked me questions about my failed relationship. It was not hard to see my heartbreak. Abuela held the three of us adults, and my two young cousins, together in our disparate struggles with her steady presence, her joy, and the mucho, mucho amor of her laughter.

Maybe it was the sobering fact of having survived the war, or the hardships endured as newcomers to the US, or maybe it was simply the passage of time that had finally softened Abuela and Papá's contentious opinions on issues of faith and religion. Back in Atiquizaya, Papá bristled whenever he learned that Abuela had taken me to mass. One day as Abuela and I made our way home through the cobblestone streets after a late mass, we found Papá pacing back and forth in front of our house enrobed in the dim light cast by the lamppost.

"¿Dónde estaban?" he asked in a rough voice. "¡Las busqué por todos lados!"

"En la iglesia," Abuela said, unconcerned.

"¿Qué, qué?" Papá could not hide his annoyance.

"¡Hombre!" shot back Abuela. "We were at church just for a little bit." In sheer frustration, Papá let his eyebrows meet in the middle of his forehead, "¡Pues, no quiero que la esté llevando a la iglesia! ¿Entiende?" he said.

If he were an animal he would have growled and snarled, but given that Abuela was his mother, he offered a stern warning instead: Don't take her to church again! Back then Papá was an ardent critic of the church. He talked about how it sided with the rich and powerful at the expense of the needy and the poor. He talked about how the pomp and ritual was designed to intimidate, how it made people fear life after death, how that focus distracted people from focusing on the now, on life as we lived it. Whatever complicated arguments Papá made against the church, what I understood growing up in Atiquizaya was that the church and religion were bad, like poison. Papá was determined to keep Camila and I from drinking any toxins. But Abuela couldn't care less what Papá thought about religion, the church, or about any of his beliefs. No argument of his was going to dissuade her from practicing her rituals or venerating her saints. Furthermore, nothing he said was going to intimidate her out of teaching me her ways.

Months rolled one on top of the other in the El Monte house with the clipped rose bushes that despite minor care yielded roses upon roses. Abuela and Papá reached a truce, and organically all six of us coalesced into a routine. November arrived, the days got shorter, and on the night of my birthday, already tucked safely in bed, my papá recounted, with as much detail as he could recall, the day I was born. After all the violence, the material lack, the loss of country, the weight of silence, the failure of his marriage, the failure of his sister's marriage, my failed relationship, the demise of family members, friends and colleagues, after all this, he found it in him to share that tender memory. Growing up Papá was never a warm man. Warmth was Mami's territory. That night, his words claimed some of the devastated terrain we shared. I was loved, his words said. Always had been.

One morning, I opened my eyes and found him standing in front of his dresser, his arms resting easily at his sides. The sun had not yet made its claim on the day; dawn lay somnolent in the corners of the room. Clothes clumped on a chair cast a deformed shape, like the shape of my inward self at the time. My two suitcases occupied a corner of the room next to Papá's homemade bookshelves, which sagged under the weight of too many books. Through the chaos and semi-darkness I could feel Papá's calm and concentration. I pretended to sleep but my mind raced ahead as the realization of what I had witnessed came into focus: Papá was praying. He stood in contemplation in front of a framed image of Saint Jude. The image had startled me when I first saw it in the room, but I said nothing. Just like he said nothing to me when he discovered my contraceptive kit one time I was visiting home from college. He unzipped it by mistake and zipped it right back up as I stood behind him holding my breath.

When I moved into the house, I had inquired about the image on his dresser and Papá said it came from Abuela. The Patron Saint of Lost Causes and Silencer of Demons had led Papá to faith again. That morning, I learned Papá was my abuela's son after all. And I learned that Papá was small, small like I was. We were both finding our way in the world, starting over again and again. Through him I saw that the ability to transcend one's limitations, self-imposed and otherwise, to reach the fullness of light after deep darkness, requires bravery and humility. Like the thaw after winter, the softening that allows the tiny crocuses to cut through the soil and greet the light, something also thawed in me that morning.

Many years in the future John and I would dream up, and eventually rebuild, a house on Dover Street. The remodeled house was constructed with a small office for me to write. The space was large enough for a desk and a small love seat. When we moved in, I covered every inch of wall space in my office with images of the Virgin of Guadalupe. I bought my first print of the Virgin in Santa Fe, New Mexico. The artist drew the Virgin with an open face, a crown on her head and a fiery red-orange aura around her body. Many other images of Our Lady eventually followed. In some, she is encircled with roses. In others, sequins adorn her robe.

After years of working as a gardener, Papá returned to El Salvador and therefore to teaching. He took advantage of the end-of-the-year school breaks to visit the United States. On one of those visits he stood at the entrance of my small office and pointed to a framed image of Guadalupe that John had brought for me from Albuquerque. Papá's face sported the topography of time's passing: deep channels on the plane of his forehead, the softer pools of his eyes, his dark hair yielding to silver. He raised a bony, trembling hand to point at the picture John had gifted me. Where did I get that one? He wanted to know. His stance was gentle and inquisitive. He was no longer the man I feared as a child.

It had been twenty-nine years since the time he'd ordered Camila and me to take our plaster virgins down from their spot on the wall above our beds. "¿Está bien bonita, verdad?" I said, looking straight at him. I did not have to defend my actions. I did not have to explain that prayer is a way to find solace, or that an image of a saint can offer resilience and hope. Abuela taught us both this. She helped us survive ourselves. He nodded and said, "Así es." I sat at my desk; he stood at the door's threshold. The suggestion of a smile registered on his face, and I could feel a smile breaking equally over mine.

I want to walk into the house that is my life and open all its doors: the pantry door, the closet doors, the bathroom doors, the porch door, the door of the cubby under the stairs. Behind each door I want to see myself reflected. I want to sit together at supper with my parents and sister like we did at each meal for years, I want to relish the company of my extended family, make and gather laughter, witness the heartbreaks unfolding, the victories earned.

I want to walk into the house that is my life and open all its doors and find myself when I was round and smooth, and tragedy and its switchblade had not yet cut through the bread of me.

I want to walk into the house that is my life and open all its doors. I am the person who loves ripe pears with gorgonzola and the English language, and I am the same person who makes sweets and jams like her abuela. I am the person Abuela taught me to be, who understands that the world is wider, wiser, and wilder than its material evidence would have us believe. When I owned my family's history I became whole again. I regained my dignity. I was no longer an object of pity. I was not ashamed. I was not a silhouette.

I want to walk into the house that is my life and open all its doors. To remember is not enough. We must speak, tell of what is remembered; only then can we take by the hand, like a small child, the phantom that roams, lost and scared, inside ourselves. Only then can we break the strings that bind us to selves who are not us.

I want to walk into the house that is my life and open all its doors. I am woman with agency, deeply loved and able to love deeply. Home is within me. I am home.

31

The Last Evening

Malabarista

A bird flew in and out of my body
back and forth, back and forth
inside and out.
With twig and feather
and threads of moonlight
she built her nest.
Patiently she sat
on her egg clutch
singing the songs
she had been taught.
When the fledglings were ready
they flew out, one by one
through the open
windows of my eyes.
Then, I reached for my pair
of red, patent leather shoes
slipped them on,
opened the front door,
and stepped out into the world.

San Salvador, El Salvador, 1980

We spent our last evening in San Salvador with Tío Javier and Mónica and their baby boy, Roberto, at their house. Conversation was hushed. Our accompaniment, the sound of sporadic gunfire. In this same room, weeks earlier, we celebrated Navidad. We feasted, danced, and laughed. In the midst of war we allowed ourselves communion.

We would leave El Salvador for the US the next morning. Tía Maura awaited us in Miami. Our flight was scheduled to depart at 9 A.M. That meant we needed to leave for the airport while the martial law–imposed sundown-to-sunup curfew was still in effect, adding another layer of risk. The four of us would make the trip alone with a hired driver in a rented van. Arrivals and departures from the airport were normally extended family affairs. Whenever Tía Maura visited, the family caravanned to pick her up from the airport and did the same to bid her good-bye. But when our departure date arrived, the extended family decided that to caravan at dawn to see us off presented too great a risk. My parents were emphatic on this point. If we got robbed, raped, disappeared, or killed, then it would happen only to the four of us.

After dinner, the adults lingered at the dining table. Their bodies spoke for them. *It is over,* said the withdrawn faces. *Over,* echoed their sagging shoulders. It had been months since Papá or Mami had dared travel to Santa Ana or Atiquizaya. Armed encounters between guerrillas and armed forces in city streets and abductions and disappearances, either by paramilitary groups or by the government, had increased exponentially.

The three extended families living in San Salvador—Tío Javier, Tía Dalia, and us—took solace in coming together every weekend. We rotated houses to host gatherings when traveling to Santa Ana to visit Abuela and Tía Salma became impossible. Those weekend lunches, spent making sopa de gallina o sopa de res, were followed by juegos de béisbol in our spacious backyard. Tío Javier was umpire, official narrator and comic relief. He insisted everyone play and organized the teams to include every household adult, as well as Tía Dalia's youngest son, still a toddler. If our dog and cat weren't skittish, Tío Javier would have handed them a bat to take part. We played with a stick and a plastic ball. The games were loud, chaotic, hilarious—a perfect release for the fear and anxiety we carried around.

We left El Salvador on Saturday, January 17, 1981. We rose in darkness and dressed in silence. Camila and I stepped into our new trousers and slipped on new blouses bought for this occasion. In the bathroom, I peeled the adhesive off a sanitary pad and attached it to my underwear. Inside my sister's light brown Mary Janes, Mami and Mónica had arranged wedges of one-hundred-dollar bills. The night before, Mami and Mónica carefully calibrated how much money Camila could carry without forcing her gait or compromising her courage. Punctually at 5:30 A.M., the man who was to drive us to the airport arrived. While he placed our four small suitcases and a cardboard box with books in the van, we stood on the sidewalk and embraced Tío Javier and Mónica. The thud of the trunk shutting told us it was time to leave.

We drove through deserted city streets. Drifted past revolutionary slogans—"Hasta la victoria siempre," "Libertad para presos políticos"—past the sprayed initials of resistance organizations: RN, ERP, FPL. The van chomped the black road underneath, bringing us closer to the lonely stretch of road where only weeks before three American nuns had been murdered. To leave meant to survive. Yet, the sense of victory lasted the length of a breath. We were leaving, but our loved ones were staying behind.

I sensed the pad between my legs. I shifted in my seat from the discomfort. The more unease I felt, the tighter I held on to the Barbie doll I carried. Camila clutched a fluffy pink elephant, a good-bye gift from Tía Dalia. My Barbie was a prized possession. I took great care of it. Tía Maura brought it to me all the way from Miami. La situación made it so Tía Maura couldn't visit us anymore. In a role reversal I was now taking the doll back to its birth country. It spoke English and I didn't. Somehow, I figured she could be an ally in our new home. The thought caused a flurry excitement. After years of wondering what the United States was like, I was going to now call it home. What toys and food awaited! What would English sound like in my voice?

The van sped forward through the light of early morning. Surely there was birdsong emanating from the plentitude of vegetation that lined the stretch from San Salvador to the airport. We rode on. From my seat I recognized trees whose crowns I knew so well: the elongated leaves of the mangoes, the oblong ones of the aguacates, the bright green ones of the guanacastes and the leggy maquilishuats, our national tree. We checked off the first highway kilometer. Then the second. There would be no triumph unless we arrived at the airport unscathed. My parents knew this. The driver knew this. I knew this. As the car sped and the scenery outside blurred, I drifted, replaying what happened the evening before.

While the adults spoke to one another in low volumes at the dining room table, Camila and I played with baby Roberto. We clapped and squealed as the newly turned one-year-old stumbled, taking tentative steps back and forth between us, and the bright yellow and orange swirls of the living room furniture echoed our fun. From the corner of my eye, I saw Mami and Mónica walk into one of the bedrooms.

"Claudia, vení para áca," Mami instructed.

"Un momento, Mami," I groaned back, not wanting to break from my game with Robertito.

When I walked into the room, Mónica grabbed my arm. She led me straight into the bathroom, then quickly snapped the door shut behind us. Mami was there waiting for me.

"¿Qué pasa?" I asked. Something obviously furtive was going on. Mónica spoke first. "Es que vos y tu Mami van a llevar algo especial," she said in a low voice, audible only in the confines of the space. Mami stepped forward, holding what appeared to be a sanitary pad.

"Mira, este es un Kotex que hemos partido a la mitad para cargar dinero," Mami said. She held up the sanitary napkin, which was split lengthwise and stuffed with American hundred-dollar bills. I looked down at the thick pad stuffed with the rectangular green pieces of paper. My parents' savings tucked in a sanitary pad. I looked up at Mami, then at Mónica. They wanted me to wear it on our way to the airport and leave it on until we were in the air. Mami had a nervous, shy, pleading look. "I'll be wearing one too," she said. In the weeks leading up to our departure my parents started to convert their entire savings from colones into dollars through the black market, paid at a higher price than the official exchange rate. The bills in Camila's shoes and in the pads Mami and I would wear accounted for almost all of my parents' entire life savings.

Yes, I would wear the pad. But I had never been on an airplane. How was I going to know, once safely airborne, when it would be safe to take the pad out? Was Mami going to tell me? Did Papá know about this? Tío Javier? I wanted to ask these questions, but I didn't. I understood that my age would keep government authorities from patting me down and certainly from searching my crotch. At least that was the hope. I understood the vulnerability of the mission. The moment engulfed me. I had been taught to make Molotov cocktails. I had to duck balazos. I had seen corpses on the street. But this was the morsel of adulthood that I had been craving, the key that would open the doors to all the intimacies adults kept between themselves. I was not going to ruin my moment by asking questions.

The bills jabbed my thighs as we walked out the house and climbed into the van. Mami and Papá sat next to each other. Camila and I sat across facing them. Every slight movement on my part conjured the money's presence. The driver turned the engine on. From my window seat I saw Mónica hold our sleeping baby cousin in one arm. We waved adíos. Mónica returned the good-bye with her free hand. Our silent bodies gave in to the van's inertia. For the first time ever, I watched Papá cry.

We were in the air before noon. I sat next to Camila. Mami and Papá sat together in the row behind us. The plane to Miami flew over a stretch of Pacific Ocean where waves crashed against volcanic black beaches. Camila complained about her shoes. I turned to Mami and asked her if it was safe to take off the pad.

"En un minuto," she said.

From my window seat I watched the lush green of our cerros and admired the consequences of their volcanic heritage rammed up against one another like sheets of corrugated metal. Gone were the weekend lunches at our house in Colonia Satélite, gone were the years under my Tía Salma's grape arbor sipping coffee and eating pan dulce as our skin glistened with sweat. I was leaving behind San Salvador, Santa Ana, Atiquizaya, our volcanoes. I was leaving behind the tragedy of Lauro's fate, his brothers and sisters, Yuri, Glenda, my extended family, my friends. I would not see Jorge again. The plane continued to make its ascent. When it reached cruising altitude Mami tapped my shoulder to let me know it was time. In the bathroom I discovered, to my surprise, spotting on the pad. My cycle had started somewhere, sometime, between the city and the airport. I pulled the bills from the pad and folded them in half as best I could. Mami was waiting outside the door to use the bathroom after me and I handed her the bills as I stepped out. In our seats, Camila discretely pulled the money out of her shoes. The plane cut through a bank of clouds, reached clear sky and the cabin flooded with sunlight.

Borrón y cuenta nueva.

Epilogue

The civil war in El Salvador singed all of us who lived through it, those who escaped it, and those who were born after it, whether in El Salvador or in the diaspora. This is my story of the war. May there be thousands more stories like it. Stories of grit and bone, stories of heart and hope, of arrival and becoming, historias de barro, de sol y luna, de balas y de maíz. Stories like this one are like seeds. We water them when we tell them, we tell them and watch ourselves flourish into the trees we carry within.

ACKNOWLEDGMENTS

I want to thank Carmen Castro Luna, Sean Heron, Leticia Hernández-Linares, Jen Marlowe, Rick Simonson, Sarah Bardeen, and Waverly Fitzgerald (RIP) for their valuable feedback to early manuscript drafts. Gracias Wendy Call for the years of encouragement and editorial direction. Deepest thanks to John Olivares Espinoza for his care, humor, and excellent editorial support.

Mil gracias a mis padres por su cariño y apoyo: Mami, Irene Luna Blanco, for the gift of teaching me to read and write, and Papá, Ramón Castro Vargas, for always being there for me and for the years of researching and culling material central to the book. Infinite gratitude to my aunt María Elena Blanco for giving us a second chance at life.

I also want to thank Hedgebrook, Centrum, and the Whiteley Center for the gift of time in residence, as well as King County's 4Culture and Jack Straw Cultural Center for their support.

I am grateful to my agent Stephanie Cabot of Susanna Lea Associates and to Marisa Siegel at Northwestern University Press.

Special thanks, con agradecimiento especial, to Salvadoran painter Jocapi, José Cándido Pineda, whose beautiful painting *Para la Paz* graces the cover.

Finally, my deepest gratitude to Sean Heron, my formidable support team of one, for the years of encouragement, thoughtful conversations, laughter, generosity, and love.

*

My poems "Visions of Gladness" and "My Father's Garden" originally appeared in *Cipota Under the Moon* (Tía Chucha Press, 2022) and *Good News* (Laney College, 2005), respectively.

An earlier version of chapter 26 first appeared as "Me encanta el Fútbol" in *Soccer America* online in 2015 (republished online in 2018).

Chapter 29 is a later version of my essay "Ex Libris," which appeared in *Puntos de Fuga / Vanishing Points*, edited by Tania Pleitez Vela, Alexandra Lytton Regalado, and Lucía de Sola (San Salvador: Editorial Kalina, 2017).

An earlier version of chapter 31 first appeared as "To Say Good-Bye" in *Jack Straw Writers Anthology*, vol. 18 (Jack Straw Cultural Center, Seattle, 2014).